Native American History

A Captivating Guide to the Long History of Native Americans Including Stories of the Wounded Knee Massacre, Native American Tribes, Hiawatha and More

Free Bonus from Captivating History (Available for a Limited time)

Hi History Lovers!

Now you have a chance to join our exclusive history list so you can get your first history ebook for free as well as discounts and a potential to get more history books for free! Simply visit the link below to join.

Captivatinghistory.com/ebook

Also, make sure to follow us on:

Twitter: @Captivhistory

Facebook: Captivating History:@captivatinghistory

Contents

Introduction

Trying to detail the history of the people of an entire continent is really an impossible task. While people talk about Native Americans, there are many tribes on both continents, and many who are know some of the history of the peoples of Central and South America are aware that many of those native peoples had empires. This was very different to the tribes of North America.

There are some native peoples who don't mind (and even prefer) being called Indians because they have become accustomed to it over the years. At the same time, they can only shake their head at how, even today, many Americans and the world at large still refuse to correct themselves when something is clearly and unequivocally wrong. Others are alright with being called Native Americans because it is closer to being accurate; but some see this as insulting because of the experiences the people have had with Americans and they do not want to be associated with the nation. Many would prefer to be known by the tribes, nations, and groups that they identify with or belong to. Just as people make a distinction between the French, English, and Germans, it is logical to address each of the native groups by their identities instead of lumping them together as a group.

Similar to talking about Europeans, when talking about the population of an entire continent it would probably be best to think of them as North Americans. However, this term is not commonly used and today also means the people who migrated (either willingly or unwillingly) to the continent. For the sake of this book, the peoples will be discussed as Native Americans to distinguish them from other groups. And they have an incredibly extensive and rich history that has largely been lost to the brutal practices and deadly diseases of Europeans and Americans.

North America is a much larger continent than Europe and its number of native groups was far more diverse than any on the European continent. There were some regions, such as the southeastern and northwestern regions, where native peoples banded together in large groups and had very structured hierarchies. Other places, particularly the Subarctic, Great Plains, and Great Basin, were populated by people who were nomadic, living off of what they could find and being more at peace with a less structured and more natural order. The many regions with different climates, terrains, and wildlife helped form the different traditions and lifestyles of the people who resided in these areas.

Tribes and nations ranged over many areas, with languages that had commonalities and various dialects that were more complex than the languages of Europe because of the sheer number of them. Some tribes and nations hated each other and others preferred peace. It was a uniquely balanced continent where the people had a close relationship with nature that was unmatched nearly anywhere else in the world. Across the North American continent, regardless of the environment, the people had struck a harmony with their surroundings, eating only what was needed and leaving little waste. Their reverence for their surroundings reflected their gratitude and close understanding of the world in which they lived.

Their reverence for nature is often mistaken as worship of nature. This is because Europeans had increasingly moved away from nature, crowding into densely populated cities and becoming largely ignorant of how to thrive or even survive in the wild. The rather unnatural draw of large numbers of people in cities had already caused several major plagues that nearly wiped out the population in

Europe. As a result, the people who survived in Europe were far more resilient to diseases that were deadly to people who were more sheltered and healthy. When Europeans decided they needed to find wealth, religious freedom, or whatever else drew them to North America, their diseases proved nearly fatal to the native peoples. This would play a significant role in their relationships over time, and, ultimately, they used it as another weapon against the natives. It is well documented that Europeans, and, later, Americans would trade disease contaminated blankets and goods with Native Americans to wipe them out, making their attacks and raids on the native peoples easier.

From the strange relationship between the natives (who were baffled by how ill-equipped Europeans were in terms of survival on the land) and the Europeans (who believed they were superior either because of their god or their "advanced technology"), some very courageous Native Americans were either born into or thrust into the spotlight. Today, people like Sacagawea, Pocahontas, and Sitting Bull are just as well-known as Washington, Jefferson, and Lincoln. There were events that happened on the continent that permanently damaged any relationship, and many of the people in Europe were incredibly critical of the treatment of the Native Americans by Americans. There have even been some mild attempts within the US and Canada to acknowledge the horrors that the governments wrought, but neither country is willing to do much to rectify the wrongs.

In the end, the people native to North America are not defined by the savage actions of the Americans, Spanish, and Canadians who stole their lands, but by their own actions. They have had leaders who tried to guide them to do right and leaders who died trying to set a good example. Even today, the native peoples continue to try to find a way forward, even as so many of them face poverty and neglect that is contrary to the agreements that resulted in them residing on reservations. Some have found a way forward and have begun to thrive and reestablish their peoples in nations that no longer resort to the same underhanded methods used against them. As the Cherokee used the court systems to press their case over a century ago, Native Americans today have learned that they can not only use the courts of the US, they can also push back on wrongs and are more likely to be heard.

Chapter 1 – Theories of the Arrival of the First Native Americans

It is impossible to know exactly how the first peoples in the Americas arrived. For years, a single theory was believed because it appeared to be the most logical explanation. However, as time went on and science became more exacting and reliable, the original idea began to be questioned because there were many problems with the theory. Just as it is difficult to know exactly what routes were taken by those earliest human civilizations in Eastern Africa to the rest of Africa, Europe, and Asia, historians are still trying to explain exactly how people arrived so far from the cradle of humanity onto two continents separated by two vast oceans.

This chapter examines the original theory of how people first arrived on two apparently remote continents and the theories that have been developing since the turn of the century.

The Long-Held Belief in the Trip across the Bering Strait

Frequently called the Bering Strait Theory or the Theory of Beringia, it has roots in a theory postulated back in the 16th century. Beginning with a Spanish missionary named Fray Jose de Acosta, the idea was first suggested in 1590. At the time, there were many debates about how the native peoples of the Americas, encountered by Spanish and

Portuguese conquistadors, originally arrived. Rejecting the original ideas presented by others, de Acosta kept with the familiar idea of walking across land, clearly disbelieving that anyone before Columbus would have been able to arrive in any other way. Of course, the Pacific Ocean and the full extent of all of South and North America were as yet unknown. However, most were aware that Asia was across the Pacific. To de Acosta, this suggested that a land bridge had been available at some point. To him, it seemed obvious that Asian hunters were the most likely to travel across any land bridge. Since none of the European philosophers and explorers of the time were aware that the northern regions were covered in ice, they thought it was plausible that land connected Asia to the new continents.

The 18th century saw a significant shift in the original theory as Russia pushed further and further east. Under Peter the Great, the czar from 1682 to 1725, explorers traversed the cold tundra to map out the complete Russian Empire. A man named Vitus Bering, a Danish explorer, was tasked with leading the expedition in the area now known as the Bering Strait region. Until his journey, this part of the map was generally shown to be land that connected with the Americas. European influence on North and South America was several hundred years old by the reign of Peter the Great, and even his maps showed the thinking of the day. And that was exactly why he wanted to find out how much of the theory was true. As he was increasing his empire, there might be a potential way for that empire to continue to expand east into North America. This would have created a Russian presence that was largely absent from the North American continent at the time.

Bering made two voyages to determine the map of the region. The first voyage was taken in 1724, the last full year of Peter the Great's reign. He would again travel the region in 1741, nearly two decades after the czar's death. What Bering found was already well-known to the Chukchi who lived in the eastern part of Russia—there was water between the Asian continent and North America. Not only that, but there had been people living across the water who traded with the Chukchi for thousands of years. This seemed to debunk de Acosta's theory that people had crossed over land. While Bering was able to help provide a more accurate map of the region's land and water, this restarted the debate in more lively terms about how North and South America had come to be populated.

Later in the century, the English explorer Captain James Cook verified what Bering had found: the existence of the land now called Alaska. During 1778, he was able to map much of the land, proving that there was not an actual landmass to connect the two continents.

By the early 1800s, many people (largely scientists and naturalists) were traveling to the area to try to figure out how the region came to be populated. Their findings indicated that people had arrived in North America much like de Acosta had suggested. These were not archeologists though, as that particular discipline did not fully develop until the early 20th century. Still, most people of European descent tried to force their findings to match what they had believed in some form or another since the end of the 16th century. It was eventually postulated that people traveled across sheets of ice between 15,000 and 12,600 years ago. Then people travelled down the coast of Canada and began to spread out in the warmer climates of both North and South America.

Often times, they would have to overlook evidence and logic to keep the Bering Strait Theory intact, but they did manage to ignore both of these until the end of the 20th century when Native Americans began to be more vocal in their disagreement.

By the early 21st century, archeologists were beginning to listen to the native peoples, punching holes in the theory and ensuring that it was never likely to be more than a theory. For the first part of the 21st century, focus was placed on the histories of those native peoples who had been on the continents thousands of years before the European explorers, who were misrepresented as being the discoverers of the land. Once people began to be more open to the histories as told by the native peoples, they were able to start developing more likely theories for how the continent came to be populated.

The Call from Native Americans to Rethink Their Origins

There are many Native Americans who call the long-held Bering Strait Theory the Bering Strait Myth. Intellectuals have spent years studying and debunking this theory that has nothing to do with the Native American legends, beliefs, and history, and looks only at the arrival of people in the Americas based on European descendant science and theories. They point out that the theory also makes the somewhat unbelievable claim that many animals and plants are said to have made the same trek through impossible climates to reach both continents.

One of the primary problems with the Bering Strait Myth is that it completely discounts all of the actual history of the people who lived on the lands long before any Europeans were aware that the continents existed. Native peoples were considered to be savage and uneducated, so their histories were largely ignored and their stories discounted. This is relatively ironic as the Europeans and people of European descent still believed in the Creation Theory, of which there was even less evidence than the Bering Strait Myth. While it is true that many Native Americans had myths regarding the beginning of the world, the myths were no less believable than the Christian myth of creation.

Even more problematic than ignoring the stories was the European inclination to ignore facts. For example, today it is known within the Mohawk Nation that they have been counting winters in North America for more than 33,000 years. By looking at the Bering Strait as the origin for people populating the continents, scientists, naturalists, and later archeologists were trying to force a narrative that ignored older findings across two entire continents. They looked at what was known as being a result of the Bering Strait Theory instead of trying to figure out the truth based on what was known based on the actual histories as told by the first inhabitants.

Instead of disregarding the actual histories of the people, Europeans and their descendants could have looked at the timelines presented by many nations to get a much more accurate idea of the history of North and South America. By ignoring it, we have literally lost hundreds of years in understanding how the people arrived and thrived. As so many native people were slaughtered during the early centuries of European conquest and empire building, it is far less likely that the truth will ever be known. Too much of the histories of the natives have been destroyed, and trying to follow the still flawed science of today is not likely to provide the insight that the histories of native peoples would have provided several hundred years ago.

As noted above, many Europeans tried to force this narrative for largely political reasons. By believing that the people who were already present were recent occupants, the Europeans felt that they had as much right to the land as the people they encountered. They were able to keep believing in Manifest Destiny because it seemed less like they were stealing and more like they were simply taking what the others had taken before them. After all, considering that they still used the misnomer of 'Indians,' it helped justify the theft by also believing that they were recent arrivals from lands comparable to India or other places in Asia. Another way for them to think about it was that the native peoples had arrived from Siberia or other European nations, and they were very accustomed to attacking other Europeans. This seemed to be more of an extension of those battles—they were also fighting with other European nations on the land anyway. Stealing the land from native peoples didn't seem like it was any more wrong than stealing it from European people who were much more recent arrivals.

This is not only tragic, but it also reduces the odds of finding the truth. Science can only prove so much, and any evidence from 30,000 years ago is going to be virtually impossible to find. Consider the two most notable landmarks from ancient times: the Egyptian Pyramids and the Great Wall of China. The Pyramids are less than 5,000 years old. The Great Wall of China is a young 2,300 years old. Since the Americas were already populated by the time both of these structures were created-—even by the timetable of the Bering Strait Myth— humanity was already very well established by the time Leif Erikson arrived; it was even more established about 400 years later when Christopher Columbus arrived. There is precious little that you can find in Europe from around the time the Egyptian Pyramids were made; it is just as unlikely to find anything in North or South America to prove the existence of people from 30,000 years ago. The histories of the people who lived on the American continents would be the best source as they actually had an understanding of their own cultures, civilizations, and how long they had occupied the land. If someone were to ignore all European history that dated back several thousand years ago, it would be virtually impossible to get a full idea of the migratory patterns of the Norsemen and Romans, let alone that of the smaller tribes and clans. In short, you really cannot discount their histories, and that is exactly why it is necessary to listen to the remaining Native Americans to get a better starting point for understanding how they arrived and populated the lands.

Following the Evidence Instead of a Preconceived Narrative

With so many native peoples slaughtered or forced off their lands to die in regions where they had never been before, much of the history of the peoples in North and South America has been lost. Although it was not strange that those of European descent ignored the natives, it is strange that they tended to ignore the expertise of geologists. Not only did the native peoples disagree with the Bering Strait theory, but geologists have also often been vocal about how the icecaps of Alaska, Canada, and the Pacific Northwest would have made it impossible for humans to survive. Based on studies done in the early 21st century, many scientists and archeologists are now willing to acknowledge that the Bering Strait Theory was simply not possible. There is evidence that people were present on the continents more than 15,000 years ago. It would not have been possible for hunters to cross the ice because at the time the Bering Strait was not frozen over. When the Bering Strait was frozen over, less than 13,000 years ago, the area was too hazardous for humans to survive. The cold would have been too much to sustain human life. Ultimately, the theory originating with de Acosta became less and less accepted within the scientific community because it was obvious that humans did not amble across on foot—there was no land and they would not have survived on the ice at the time.

With the long-believed theory apparently debunked because of lack of evidence or scientific backing, debate began again as to how exactly people had arrived on the continents.

Taking a look at the evidence, scientists and archeologists have been spending more time looking at the facts rather than trying to force a narrative. Over the last decade or so, that evidence has included two very interesting findings. The first intriguing finding was evidence of mammoth hunting in Florida that appears to have occurred about 14,500 years ago. Even older is the evidence of a civilization, or perhaps more accurately a settlement, located all the way south in Chile, South America. This is far earlier than would have been possible if the ice-bridge had been the method for the arrival of the inhabitants because the water was not frozen during that time period.

Currently, scientists are looking at the theory that people traveled in a way more similar to the Europeans, such as Leif Erikson. Evidence suggests that the native peoples arrived along the shores further south and began to move inland, just at the Europeans did thousands and thousands of years later. This will be difficult to research as the coasts have been eroded and changed significantly over thousands of years, and there were and are active volcanoes and seismic activity along the western coast. Much of the evidence has likely been entirely lost to the oceans since the native peoples first arrived and began to thrive on the continents.

It is with a sense of irony that scientists are constantly verifying the histories of the original peoples. There are still some people who are trying to force the Bering Strait narrative to work, and simply apply it years earlier. Others are starting to notice the alignment of the calendars of ancient peoples with what they are continually finding in the ruins and remains. Given that there are artifacts that are much older in lower regions, it is much more likely that the first peoples arrived in multiple regions from several different locations on both sides of the ocean.

Currently, there are three possible theories for how the original people arrived. Based on the finding of human remains, dubbed the Kennewick Man, in Washington State, there is a case being made that the peoples of that region may have come from Japan. The body is similar to the Japanese Ainu people, and because Japan is an island, the people would have been able to build durable ships to cross the Pacific Ocean. In the eastern parts of the United States, tools were found that strongly resemble tools used by the Solutrean, a European group. It is possible that people traveled from Europe thousands of years ago and remained. Perhaps the most obvious answer is the correct one: people who left Europe and Asia could have populated both continents, crossed the oceans, and settled in the new land. This is still going on today, and it was something that Europeans did hundreds of years ago; so it seems strange to believe that this migration is new. Perhaps people have been coming to the Americas to escape persecution and problems over the same routes for tens of thousands of years. It will be incredibly difficult to find the truth, if not entirely impossible. However, human nature has not changed very much in 30,000 years. The answer may be that people from several continents made the trek across the ocean hoping for a better life, and that has not changed no matter how much time passes.

Chapter 2 – Current Understanding of Similar and Rival Tribes Based on Region

While it is difficult to know how the Native Americans began to populate the Americas, it is much easier to understand the societies that existed when the Europeans arrived and began to fan out over the continents. Many tribes and empires were based on the regions where they lived. In South and Central America, tribes tended to band together in one area to create empires that were relatively similar to those established in Europe. North America tended to be populated by people who preferred a more nomadic lifestyle.

North American tribes are all unique, just as the peoples of the different nations and provinces of Europe are unique. Also like Europe, it is easy to categorize the tribes and peoples based on where they lived. The land dictated much about the lives of those who occupied it, and the way that they interacted with the land tended to be a commonality that many tribes had with each other based on their locations.

Today, tribes are generally studied based on their regions as where the tribes lived would have helped to shape their beliefs and daily lives. Ten regions are used to define the types of native people who resided in them:

- Arctic

- Subarctic

- Northeast

- Southeast

- Plains

- Southwest

- Great basin

- Northwest coast

- Plateau

- California

These different regions are examined more closely in the following chapters. This chapter looks at the Native Americans in North America, regardless of their locations. Keep in mind that these are designations assigned by people of European descent and should be taken as such. These could accurately be considered incredibly oversimplified ideas of who the natives were based on the superiority complex of the Europeans and their proclivity for being dismissive of people who were not obviously of European descent. It is more akin to a child trying to understand adult concepts without actually consulting any adults to gain an accurate understanding. Still, with so many peoples either completely wiped out or with lives significantly affected by the changes they have undergone in the last few hundred years, it is at least a starting point for providing a way to categorize the original inhabitants in a way that helps foster a greater interest in the people who once thrived in North America.

A Host of Terms to Define Themselves

Because of Columbus's inability to distinguish between India and a completely different continent, the misnomer Indian has been so prevalent when referring to the natives in North America that it is often startling to imagine someone of Indian descent when the term is used.

Naturally, Native Americans have always had their own terms to identify who they are. Some of them were in tribes, but many other terms had more comparable terms within the European language than the word tribe. Some were more like nomadic bands who lived off of the land, relocating when the seasons changed. Others are more accurately described as nations, with well-established social structures and economies.

Some natives knew multiple languages, just like the peoples of Europe, and they communicated with their neighbors. Some Native American peoples had complex social structures with multiple leaders and one primary leader. They were far more complex than the one-dimensional depiction that has been associated with them for centuries. Just as there was a wealth of ways to describe the peoples of the different countries in Europe, the Native Americans were just as diverse and intriguing with their own terms to define who they were and their complex relationships with each other. This book will work to define the different peoples by the terms and identifications that they had for themselves. The term tribe will be used when it is unclear how a collective group defined themselves.

Defining the Peoples by Their Language

The chapters in the following sections describe the different peoples based on the regions where they originally lived; however, some are best described by the languages they spoke. For larger Native American nations, language was the common denominator, more so even than location. Four particular nations tend to be defined more by the languages spoken because the language was prevalent across multiple regions.

The people who spoke Algonquian included more than 100 different tribes. This particular language spread across nearly the entire nation, including some of the best known Native American tribes, such as the Blackfeet, Mohicans, and Cheyenne. The common language was also known to people outside of these tribes because of how wide-spread the language was.

The smallest group of peoples of the four defining languages is the Apache. Given how well-known the group's name still is today, they have a place in history that is better known than many of the smaller tribes who had a language that was less commonly used. Although only six tribes spoke Apache, they played a large role in the development of the cultures where they lived.

The Iroquois League was also small, and all of the native speakers were located in the Northeastern portion of what is now the United States and lower parts of Canada. It also included only six nations (Cayuga, Mohawk, Oneida, Onondaga, Seneca, and Tuscarora, who joined later in the alliance). The reason the Iroquois League is still well-known today is that they were among the first native peoples to establish longer-term relationships with the Europeans.

The final group better known by their language than their location were the members of the Sioux Nation. Like the Iroquois League, the Sioux Nation was located in a single location, though it was the Great Plains instead of the US northeast. The Sioux Nation includes three primary groups: the Eastern Dakota, Lakota, and Western Dakota.

All four of these languages will be discussed more in the following chapters, as the four languages played an important role in the cultures where they were common.

A Closer Relationship with Nature

One thing that most Native Americans had in common, regardless of their location in North or South America, was respect and reverence for nature. They had a close relationship with the land that they lived on, and it was best expressed by the saying, "We are the land." They did not see themselves as separate from the land, nor did they feel compelled to tame the land as was the thought process of many Europeans.

Not fully understanding the relationship between the Native Americans and the land, many Europeans often misunderstood it as a part of their religion. However, there is a similar concept in Christianity, best summed up with the saying "Ashes to ashes, dust to dust." While Europeans saw themselves as being separate from the Earth while they were alive, Native Americans never saw themselves as different either in life or in death. This belief was prevalent among many of the native peoples across two continents, though to different degrees. Native Americans in Central and Southern America built large structures, some that were pyramids and more complex structures. The Native Americans in North America tended to stay closer to the land, opting to live in longhouses, huts, and homes that were either part of the Earth or directly on the ground instead of erecting large structures that would separate them from it. Peoples like the Zapotec in southern Mexico believed that they were people of the sky, so the higher-ranking people lived on higher ground to be closer to their ancestors. This was not the case for the peoples in North America. The beliefs and homes of the many different peoples are detailed further in their respective chapters.

Chapter 3 – Arctic and Subarctic Tribes and Nations

When most people think about Native Americans, they often imagine people with comfortable-looking leather outfits, long braids, and beautiful expansive green lands. The peoples who live in the arctic and subarctic locations are thought of differently. Easily the most widely-known (at least in the US) term associated with the native people who lived in the frozen regions of North America is Eskimos. However, this term is neither accurate nor does it include a majority of the people who natively live in these regions.

An Expansive Stretch of Inhospitable Lands

There is no doubt that the regions labeled the arctic and subarctic are staggeringly beautiful. With vast stretches of snow and ice, you would think that it is a frozen desert where few people, if any, could survive.

These two regions are distinctly different, although it can be difficult for most people to understand the distinction between them (much like the difficulty of understanding the differences between the steppe and desert). Closer examination shows that the differences between these two regions helped to shape the lives of the peoples who lived there, just as they still control and shape the lives of people who live there today.

The Arctic – A World of Ice and Beauty

Covering some of the coldest inhabited lands in the world, the arctic is uninviting to nearly everyone except those who have lived there for centuries or millennia. As scientists and archeologists began to realize how unlikely the Land Bridge Myth was, they helped to shed more light on the people who chose to live in a place that seemed so hostile to life. The uppermost part of modern-day Greenland, Canada, and Alaska are considered the lands of the Arctic tribes. There are no trees here, and trying to grow food is nearly impossible in the frozen soil.

It is from this region that the term Eskimo arose. The term itself is from the language of the native peoples, and it can be translated as the "eater of raw meat." Today, they are more accurately known as the Inuit. The region also includes one other tribe, the Aleut. Both tribes followed one of the few sources of food, animals, living very nomadic lives. As polar bears, seals, and other animals migrated to find new sources of food, the Inuit and Aleut would follow them. This continuous movement is the reason why their territory covered so much inhospitable land area. Aleut who lived closer to the subarctic terrain tended to be more settled, establishing fishing villages as a more stable and predictable source of food.

The language of both of these peoples is known as the Eskimo-Aleut language because the two tribes had much in common. Their homes were dome-shaped, although all but the houses furthest north were made of timber and soil instead of ice. Both tribes used the skin of otters and seals to create weather-proof clothing that would keep them warmer in the forbidding climate. They used dogsleds as a faster mode of transportation across the snow and ice, and dogs were a part of nearly all of the native groups, whether migratory or stationary.

These people are truly adaptable, having been able to survive for thousands of years in regions that seemed unable to sustain human life. Their religion reflects their reverence for nature. Both Inuit and

Aleut follow the doctrine of animism, which says that every living thing has a soul, contrary to the limited belief of Christianity that only humans have souls. Their belief extends to any natural phenomena, such as thunderstorms and snow, as well as geographical features, such as mountains and rivers. Their religion was largely dominated by Shamanism. Comparable to a priest, a shaman acted as a medium between the world people could see and the next world. They were more active in working with spirits. Different regions of the Arctic held different beliefs within Shamanism. The peoples to the northeast held the mother of sea animals, Sedna, in greatest esteem. Those of the western region placed emphasis on the Moon God Igaluck (or Anningan). All of their mythologies included tricksters and those with mischievous intent.

The Native Americans in the arctic region were adept at making sculptures, working with the ivory of walrus tusks and whalebone to create a wide range of tools and accessories. The animal and nature masks used by the shamans are beautiful and show off the abilities of the people who lived in such a harsh land. Despite the difficulties of living in the freezing climates, the people made some very elegant works of art that are still remarkable now.

Today, the Native American people living in Alaska make up roughly 1.5 percent of the population. While they were protected from much of the expansion and theft of land common in the southern regions, the exposure to the travelers from those southern areas proved largely fatal to the native peoples. Like many other regions, the natives living in the arctic region did not have the necessary immunity to fight off the particularly viral diseases carried by those of European and Eurasian descent. The people of European and Russian descent who established themselves in the region did not regard the natives as being the rightful people of the land on which they had lived for millennia. Skirmishes and battles continually pushed native peoples from their lands. Oppressing them and stealing their crucial food resources further reduced the number of native peoples. It was estimated that there are today only 4.5 million native people in Alaska, up from the estimated 2,500 believed to have survived European oppression and theft in 1867 when the United States purchased Alaska from Russia.

The Subarctic – Stunning Signs of Life and Comfort

While still extremely cold, the subarctic area is able to sustain plant life. Taiga, or piney forests, stretch across the landscape, providing more food for the animals that live there. The region covers most of Canada and a large portion of Alaska. The summers are always short, and the winters are long and cold. There are also swampy areas and high plateaus that shape different parts of the region.

Two primary languages were spoken across the region. To the west, the Native Americans spoke Athabaskan, including the Deg Xinag, Gwich'in, Han, Kaska, Sekani, and Tsattine. There are several unique dialects spoken by small portions of the populations, and these dialects were not always entirely similar. The eastern section of the subarctic spoke Algonquian, including the Cree, Naskapi, and Ojibwa. It was not identical to the Algonquian spoken elsewhere, but the languages are similar enough that the people from the two different regions were able to communicate. Fewer than 65,000 people spoke these languages. While the region is able to sustain trees and a greater variety of animal life, it is still far harsher and colder than is comfortable for many people. Some of the peoples who lived in subarctic had nations that stretched much further south.

Traveling around the subarctic was difficult and required additional equipment to move from one place to another. While many tribes settled in one place, there were many who continued to migrate, following caribou and other large game. To do this they used snowshoes and toboggans. Lightweight canoes were also used when they reached bodies of water. Their homes were necessarily lightweight as well, including tents that were easy to erect and take down. When it became too cold for such lightweight homes, they settled into locations underground.

There are signs that people began to populate the region before 5000 BC. By the time the Europeans arrived, the cultures and traditions of the people were well established. With large numbers of wildlife with durable skins, the Europeans would play a much earlier role in the subarctic region. Trapping and trading with Native Americans began to change the way the Native Americans lived, and Europeans began to take over the lands that proved to be prosperous because of those very animals who had helped the Native Americans establish stable lives for millennia. As Europeans moved into the region, claiming the land, they began to kill animals at a rate that was too rapid to sustain. The large populations of the native animals were decimated, and there were fewer places for the Native American people to live and travel without incurring the anger of the invading Europeans.

Chapter 4 – Northeastern and Southeastern Peoples

The northeastern and southeastern regions were the first places where Europeans landed in what would be the United States. At first, those interactions were innocuous, with the first being well before Christopher Columbus bumbled into the New World. While it is not known what interaction, if any, occurred during the arrival of the first Europeans, history has a much greater record for subsequent interactions after the Spanish and Portuguese started invading the Caribbean, Mexico, Central and South America.

These earliest two regions were the first to see exactly what kind of threat the Europeans could pose. The crowded, crime-ridden, disease-plagued cities and towns of Europe had meant that the people living there had developed much hardier immune systems. Because of the living conditions that they were accustomed to, the Europeans were immune to the diseases that they brought with them, an immunity that the native peoples who were close to nature and kept a balance with their world did not have. Nor did the Native Americans have the same individual greed and selfishness that plagued Europe. Most of the people coming from Europe were looking for riches, power, or a place to worship freely. The last was not nearly so innocuous as it sounds because the Europeans who came looking for religious freedom tended to be the most condescending and cruel to the native peoples who had helped them survive. While accepting the help of the native peoples, many of these "good Christians" looked down on them and quickly forgot just how much the native peoples had done for them. Not all Europeans did; however, coupled with the greed and desire for power, religion became a tool for many for the extermination of those Native Americans who were not killed off by the deadly European diseases.

The Peoples of the Northeast – Settled and Cultured

The region under the subarctic region located along the northeastern coast of the US is called the Northeastern woodlands. Reaching all of the way down to modern-day North Carolina and west to the Mississippi, the peoples of this area were incredibly different to the tribes in the other regions of what later became the United States. But because these were the people the Europeans encountered when they first arrived, much more is known about the tribes both in the northeastern and southeastern sections of the country than other native peoples. Toward the western edge of the region the trees give way to the plains. Buffalo were common in this region, and the tribes in this region often interacted with the tribes of the Great Plains. The Appalachian Mountain Range and Great Lakes are two defining features. Much more temperate than their northern neighbors, the tribes were less mobile in the Eastern regions of North America.

The Native Americans in the northeastern section are divided into two main groups based on the two languages spoken when the Europeans arrived: those who spoke Iroquoian and those who spoke Algonquian. It is estimated that there were around two million native peoples in the region when the Europeans began to settle in North America.

The Iroquois Nation included a number of tribes, such as the Cayuga, Erie, Oneida, Onondaga, Seneca, and Tuscarora. These tribes primarily lived near the numerous bodies of water that were teeming with fish and wildlife. They were a highly civilized people who had fortified villages with an established system of government. Living along water, the Iroquois speakers tended to use canoes made of elm because the wood was more stable, although they were also slower than the Algonquian's canoes.

The Algonquian speakers spread well beyond just the northeastern region into the subarctic and Great Plains regions. Tribes who spoke Algonquian in the region included the Delaware, Fox, Menominee, Pequot, Shawnee, and Wampanoag. There were higher concentrations of them along the ocean where they fished for much of their food. They preferred to travel in light canoes made of birch.

Beyond Mere Survival

The peoples that the British would first encounter were not savages with a tenuous grasp on survival. Quite the opposite, these people had a much better understanding of how to live with the land and survive in a world that had four distinct seasons, unlike the settlers from England. The peoples who lived in the Northeast region understood more advanced methods of agriculture, and they had an incredibly rich culture.

Most of the Native Americans in this region farmed, with corn being a primary product of their more agrarian lifestyle. They also gathered foods from the forest and surrounding area. To ensure the soil would be rich following harvesting, they would use slash-and-burn to provide additional nutrients. They were also hunters and fishermen.

Evidence shows that these people had thrived in the region for no less than 12,000 years, and it is likely that they migrated up from the southern regions of the continent. They not only harvested crops and had a thorough understanding of the seasons to get the best yield out of the crops, they created pottery and had burial ceremonies for their dead. They had a rich culture with artisans who were adept at creating copper tools, and they had their own traditions.

Trade was common between the different tribes, which was made easier by the fact that there were only two primary languages. The Iroquois seemed to have more corn and other agrarian products to trade with the Algonquian for their animal products. They also traded their tools, pottery, and artisan items.

The Real First Europeans

Long before the English arrived with disease and a desire to take over, Norse travelers reached the region. Viking Erik the Red had helped establish what is thought to have been the first settlement in modern-day Greenland. Leif Eriksson was his son. It is thought that Eriksson lost his way returning home to Greenland after visiting Norway and arrived in North America (around 1000 AD). He and his men explored the location where he made landfall, calling it Vinland based on the impressive wild grapes that were thriving in the region even during the fall and winter. They spent the winter there, then returned to Greenland. Some scholars believe that it wasn't Leif Eriksson but an Icelandic trader named Bjarni Herjulfsson who was the first European to visit the region of North America (986 AD). There are stories that he made the trek 14 years before Eriksson journeyed to Norway and that it was Herjulfsson's tales that influenced Eriksson's stories years later. While it was clearly an interesting story, the people of Greenland did not have any desire to return, conquer, or settle in North America.

However, that was the first time any European made the trip. It is ironic that people, largely thought of as Vikings, who are commonly described as barbaric, cruel, and prone to raiding the villages and towns of Europe, were the ones who left the lands alone. Clearly it was a better place for farming and was much easier living than where the Vikings lived at the time, yet these people left the new territory alone. Ironically, the Spanish, Portuguese, and British who considered themselves so civilized and advanced had practices that were just as barbaric as the people they called savages. While the native peoples were trying to defend their traditions and lands, the newcomers slaughtered, stole, and committed genocide against them, largely because of greed. It is incredibly unlikely that any tribes who encountered Eriksson or any of the other people from Greenland would have remembered much of the encounter hundreds of years later.

The Peoples of the Southeast – Organized and Civilized

Another irony is that some consider the southeastern portion of the US to be slower to progress today. Prior to the arrival of the British, this region was perhaps the most like many of the European countries. The native peoples had hierarchies, laws, and governments that made the southeastern area civilized and structured in ways that were more familiar to the Europeans. It took much more to over-look the advanced culture of these people than in the other areas because they were much more easily able to adapt the European ideas and integrate those ideas into their own.

The region stretched from the inner part of present-day Virginia down to Florida. It stretched west to modern-day Texas. It is a much smaller division than the other three covered so far, but it was far more advanced in terms of settlements, laws, and hierarchy.

The southeastern region was the most fertile and had the best growing season as the seasons were longer. Constant rains helped the Native Americans in the southeast region settle down and develop advanced agrarian civilizations. The range of crops included squash, tobacco, maize, many species of beans, and sunflowers. Like in many agrarian regions of Europe, their lives were based on an agrarian culture. With a better understanding of the land and nature, they were able to find the right kinds of plants for the diverse range of soil types. While they relied on farming for most of their food, there were still hunters and fishermen to provide the necessary meat.

There was one primary language for the southeastern area, the Muskogean language. Although there were many tribes, five main nations were present: Cherokee, Chickasaw, Choctaw, Creek, and Seminole. They each spoke their own variation on the Muskogean language that was broken down into several different dialects. Compared to the other regions, this area was easily one of the most densely populated.

An Annual Celebration

As a heavily agrarian people, they participated in many celebrations and festivals based on the seasons. The Green Corn Festival was one that had great significance to the people. Held in the fall, the shaman for each tribe and the warriors would dance around the fire, corn in their hands. The corn was cooked as an offering to the spirits.

Following the dance, the natives would create a second fire and corn would be cooked for everyone present. They then ate and danced, much like European harvesting ceremonies, such as October Fest. Though the winters were mild to non-existent (snow is still a rare sight in the region), it was a time when the natives would spend more of the day in their homes.

When Their Rich, Fertile Lands Were Used Against Them

These lands that established some similarities to European culture ended up being a significant draw for the new arrivals. Ignoring the obvious social hierarchies and cultural similarities, the colonials (and later Americans) wanted those rich, fertile lands for themselves. While there were some Native Americans who were not welcoming, there were many who aided the early settlers, showing them what they needed to know so that they did not suffer the same fate as Roanoke. The "civilized" Europeans soon realized that the natives in this region had the best resources of any area explored by the Europeans to that point. Many of the Europeans and early Americans did not want to share with the natives, so they justified genocide and theft through any means necessary, including their religion, Christianity. Clearly failing to understand the teachings of Jesus and the Ten Commandments that should have dictated their behavior, Europeans and Americans chose not to apply their religion and commandments to the native peoples. Instead they used their religion to justify killing the native peoples and laying claim to their lands.

Exposure to the Europeans decimated the numbers of Native Americans whether due to outright killing, disease, or theft of their land. Within 300 years of their arrival, the Europeans would finally push the remaining native peoples off of the land that had been their home for longer than any of the modern-day European nations have existed. Even when considering the Italian roots, the native peoples in the Southeastern region were several thousand years older. They were more established than Egypt. Yet some Americans proved their ultimate barbarity when, within less than 75 years of the nation's existence, they forced the Cherokees from their lands along the Trail of Tears.

As will be explored in more depth later, there was a single set of native peoples that did successfully fight off the invading settlers of British descent. After the US had forced millions of Native Americans off of their land, including the Cherokee along the Trail of Tears, the Seminole Tribe refused to be forced off their lands in the same way. Using tactics that were similar to the ones the native peoples had taught the colonists during the War for Independence, the Seminole found ways to hide and escape removal. There were small pockets of people from the Cherokee Nation who succeeded through similar means, but a much larger portion of the Seminole who were supposed to leave Florida remained.

Chapter 5 – Plains and Plateau Peoples

The Native Americans who were initially spared the greed of Europeans and Americans lived in ways that people more closely associate with the native peoples in North America. More along the lines of the stereotypical "Indian," the peoples of the plains and plateaus were adept hunters. First Europeans, and later Americans, would initially befriend the natives as they needed to cross their territories and understand the lands. Of course, the first Europeans and Americans to cross the plains and plateaus were interested in the money they could make from trapping and hunting, but eventually, they would look at the land itself as being highly desirable since it was relatively easy to survive in these areas. The problem was that survival was easy; profiting from the territories would prove to be much harder than any of the Americans had initially anticipated.

The Great Plains – Where the Buffalo and Humans Lived in Harmony

The Great Plains was the most expansive region south of the freezing lands of the subarctic, and Native Americans lived across it in the prairies. Stretching from the Mississippi River on the eastern border to the Rocky Mountains on the west, and southern Canada on the north to the Gulf of Mexico to the south, it was a region that was home to many different tribes and nations.

The peoples of this region spoke five primary languages; Algonquian, Athabaskan, Caddoan, Siouan, and Uto-Aztecan. The use of these languages spread well beyond the boundaries of the plains region. Because the territory touched on six other regions, the peoples in this area were able to communicate with a much wider group than any of the other native peoples.

When people depict Native Americans, the peoples of the Great Plains are typically the image that is pictured. Riding horses to hunt down buffalo across vast areas meant that a number of tribes were nomadic. However, there were more settled peoples who farmed and thrived on the lands currently used for the same purposes by large companies today. Their teepees and elaborate feather headdresses were integral parts of their lives. Teepees were made with durable buffalo hide and were easy to take down and erect while they were hunting.

When Europeans brought horses to North America, the tribes and nations on the Great Plains quickly became experts on how to raise and ride the animals. They could more easily hunt on horseback, making them very formidable hunters and warriors. It also resulted in more people becoming nomadic as they could more easily chase down herds that had previously been too fast or too difficult to follow across vast distances on foot.

The Tribes

With such an expansive region to live in, there were many tribes, some of whom also resided in other regions. Well-known people such as the Arapaho, Cheyenne, Otoe, Shawnee, Cree, Sioux, Pawnee, Blackfoot, and Crow occupied portions of the Great Plains and other surrounding regions. Lesser known tribes include the Gros Ventre, Kiowa, Mandan, Iowa, Kansa, Omaha, and Ponca.

When Americans forced native peoples off of their lands in the east, they were initially moved to the Great Plains. Peoples of the Cherokee Nation ended the Trail of Tears in the area and never fully recovered. Although the space was fertile and the weather adequate for farming, similar to the kind of life the Cherokee had lived before being forced off of their lands, the soil was not anything like that of the southeastern region.

The Primary Natural Resource

Buffalos were an important resource to the native peoples, and every part of a buffalo was used after it was killed. From their skins used for homes to their bones used for tools to their meat used for food, Native Americans were very resourceful and appreciative of these large animals. The animals were essential to the daily lives of the people, so the buffalo were only killed based on the need. Native Americans did not hunt them for trophies or kill more than they could use. Hunters would use teepees during the hunts because they were simple to use and easy to set up.

Soon the native peoples came to be seen as a hindrance to western expansion; the US government took the tactic of slaughtering the greatest resource on the plains—the bison. It was an intentional act on the part of the US to force the people to give up their traditional way of life.

The Plateau – A Peaceful People along the Numerous Rivers

The Plateau region, also known as the Columbia Plateau, stretched along the eastern portion of the Pacific Northwest. The native peoples lived in modern-day Canada and eastern Washington and Oregon (east of the Cascade Mountains) and stretched as far as western Montana. Although the region is largely steppe, many rivers wind through the territories, including the second longest river in North America, the Columbia River.

Living along the lively river, the people were mostly peaceful. Most of the roughly dozen tribes that lived in this region were settled, getting everything they needed from the rivers where they lived. Trout and salmon were a major part of their diet, but they also hunted animals that were drawn to the water. There was also plenty of plants, berries, and nuts.

Two primary languages of the region were Penutian and Salishan. The vast majority of tribes spoke their own versions of these languages though, so communication was not as straightforward as it might initially appear. Still, they did communicate and largely remained at peace until the Americans arrived.

The people did not tend to form large, populous areas, opting to remain in smaller, easy to sustain settlements. Despite the relatively small area of the Columbia Plateau, there were roughly a dozen tribes. The names of most of these tribes are known only to the people who live in the region today, such as the Columbia, Klamath, Klickitat, Modoc, Nez Perce, Salish, Skitswish, Spokane, Yakima, and Walla Walla.

Just like today, the climate was incredibly varied, with warm summers and snowy winters. During the warmer months, the people enjoyed living near the water to quickly cool off after a hard day's work, as well as to fish for salmon. During the winter months, they would live underground. These underground homes, called pit houses, were often connected through tunnels.

The Arrival of Horses

When horses became common to the people of the Great Plains, the tribes of the Columbia Plateau became partners in the raising and training of this animal. There is evidence that there was a type of horse that had been indigenous to North America, but it had died out long before the Europeans arrived. With the reintroduction of a large creature that could make daily life easier, the native peoples in the Columbia Plateau were quick to help their neighbors in using horses.

Given that much of the travel in this region was done on water, there was less of a need for horses in the plateaus. However, the animal did make it easier to travel over the large stretches of steppe that had previously been too barren for the natives to travel regularly.

Horses became important for hunting in the Great Plains, they helped the Native Americans of the Columbia Plateau to expand their hunting grounds and act as traders with the encroaching Europeans. With the arrival of Lewis and Clark, European diseases began to take a toll on these previously thriving people. It should have been a signal that the people who appeared well-meaning were not as innocuous as they seemed. Nor were they backed by a government that would honor anything that Lewis and Clark promised. Like the Great Plains natives, horses would provide help for the Columbia Plateau peoples, but also like the Great Plains natives, the joint effort was not enough to overcome those Americans who cared only about self-enrichment.

Adept with Weapons

Despite being a largely peaceful region, weapons were essential to every tribe in the plateau. Farming was not very common in this region, so hunters played a vital role in the survival of every tribe. As a result, their weapons were incredibly effective, particularly ranged weapons.

Lassos were a common tool and helped to bring down larger game. The natives also used spears and harpoons to help during more difficult hunts. Of course, their most effective and relied-upon weapon was the bow and arrow.

Even with all of these tools at their disposal, the natives were not always successful at taking down animals as often as needed, and that is when they used cunning. Fire was used to smoke out the animals or drive them into areas where other hunters were waiting. Some hunters would also drive animals into the water where they would be much easier to catch and kill.

Back at their homes, knives and worn-down pebbles were used to skin the animals and prepare the hides. The pebble tool was much hardier and functional than the name suggests. It was used not only for preparation, but chopping, cutting, and pulping as well.

Chapter 6 – The Great Basin and Southwestern Regions

Both of these regions were somewhat small, but they were home to many native peoples living very different lifestyles. This was in large part because of how diverse the terrain was. The Great Basin and Southwestern regions include today's Grand Canyon, Las Vegas, and many other well-known current attractions. The modern-day state of Texas touched both of these regions, and it stretched just shy of the ocean, stopping at the California region.

The Great Basin – A Harsh Terrain with Progressive People

The people who lived in the Great Basin had the Rocky Mountains along its eastern border and the Sierra Nevadas to the west. To the north was the Columbia Plateau and the Colorado Plateau on the southern end. It remains a largely inhospitable area of salt lakes that do not allow life, the desert, and other harsh natural features. Still it was home to a large number of native peoples.

The two primary dialects of the regions were Shoshonean and Uto-Aztecan. Given the harsh terrain, few of the people living were in a settled area, preferring to remain constantly on the move to find the optimal living spaces during the very hot summers and freezing winter nights.

Food sources were largely what could be found in those very harsh conditions, such as lizards, snakes, and other small animals. They also ate nuts, roots, and seeds. Their homes matched their nomadic lifestyles, and tribes moved with wikiups (wigwams) that were made largely from saplings, leaves, and willow poles. Their social structures were what could be expected from a nomadic people, and the leaders of each tribe were largely informal leaders.

Given the harsh terrain and how difficult survival was, there was little reason for the native peoples to worry about the kinds of invasions and hostile takeovers that occurred in the other regions. Had gold not been discovered, it would likely have remained that way. Unfortunately, once Americans heard that gold had been discovered in the region, they applied Manifest Destiny to the Great Basin because it had resources that they wanted. Treaties were again broken with the native peoples, and they were pushed onto lands where survival was far more difficult.

A More Open Lifestyle

The people of the Great Basin were incredibly intelligent and progressive in their approach to life. They understood the preciousness of life. To survive in such harsh terrain, they were experts in the land and the areas surrounding it, even areas well outside it. One of the most famous of the Shoshone was Sacagawea, who played a vital role in the success of Lewis and Clarke's expedition across the Louisiana Purchase. They knew many different languages and knew how to survive in some of the most challenging conditions in what is now known as the United States.

Like many other Native American groups, women were seen as equals and were treated as such, unlike European women and American women. Young people were allowed to explore their sexuality without stigma, which could result in a trial marriage period. If a marriage was not working out, either one of the spouses needed only to return to their parents' home for the couple to be divorced.

Given how harsh the terrain was and the reality that women could die in childbirth, women were allowed to marry two men, typically two brothers. Called fraternal polyandry, this practice helped to keep the tribes and bands small so that life could be easily sustained in the difficult environment.

The Beginning of the Ghost Dance

The Great Basin natives were incredibly thankful for what the land gave them. As a result, they had two main ceremonies: called the Ute Bear Dance and the Sun Dance. These dances would eventually inspire the Ghost Dance. Seen as a way of helping the native people reconnect with their spiritual beliefs and disavow the lifestyle of Americans, it would eventually be seen as a threat to Americans instead of being seen for what it was. The ceremonies and beliefs of the Great Basin natives would inspire others until Americans decided they should be outlawed. As a result, thousands of native peoples would be killed as they tried to return to their traditional ways, all because some Americans could not take the time to understand the people they had wronged so many times before the end of the 19th century.

The Southwest – Two Ways of Living

The southwestern region stretches from the western part of Texas on the eastern boundary and all the way to Arizona on the west. It spreads as far north as modern-day Colorado and Utah, and all the way south into present-day Mexico. Though this region is not nearly as vast as the native territories to the east or the Great Plains, many tribes lived there, each adapting to the location where they lived.

Unlike many of the other regions, the people who lived in the southwestern areas were far less similar to each other. Also unlike the fate of most of the Native Americans who were constantly betrayed by the US, the peoples of the southwestern region were victims to the indifference and cruel practices of the Spanish. While those of British descent often broke treaties they had with the Native

Americans and took their lands, those of Spanish descent treated the people of the southwestern region the same as they had treated the Aztec, Zapotec, Incans, and Mayans; either the people were slaughtered or enslaved. The people of Spanish did not regard the native people as people, so killing them for their resources was not considered a sin against their god. By the time the Mexicans lost the region to the US, the tribes of this region had already been all but decimated. Once the land became part of the US, those native peoples who had survived the Spanish genocide were moved onto reservations by the US government.

Villagers and Farmers

Some of the most varied types of housing were used in this region. The natives living in the southern regions did not have the wealth of large game that resulted in easily movable homes like the peoples of the Great Planes, Columbia Plateau, or eastern regions. Instead, they used the land for their homes. Like the people of South and Central America, the Native Americans living in the southwest were farmers and needed sturdier homes during the scorching summers. Their domiciles are called pueblos, and they are more akin to apartment complexes than single homes. Some were carved into the rocks and caverns. However, most of the pueblos were made of stone and adobe.

These people lived a relatively structured life, with the center of their villages being more of an open, community area. The ceremonial pit houses, also called kivas, were located in the center of the villages.

Some of the most famous tribes in the region were the Hopi, Yaqui, Yuma, and Zuni. They were all adept farmers, despite the less than ideal soil.

Nomads and Warriors

The Native Americans who chose a more nomadic lifestyle were also often more violent. They moved around, living from the game they could kill and the villages that they raided. Their meat usually derived from what they were able to hunt while their vegetables and other food sources tended to come from the farms where they conducted raids. Because they were nomadic, it was difficult to predict where they would strike next.

Their homes were much easier to build and abandon when it was time to move to the next place. Constructed mainly of bark and mud, their homes were called hogans or roundhouses.

The most well-known nomadic tribes were the Apache and the Navajo.

Chapter 7 – California and Northwest Coast

All up and down the west coast was an impossible paradise before the Americans and Europeans arrived. Much like Hawaii before those of European descent invaded, this thin stretch of land next to the Pacific Ocean was stunningly beautiful for millennia. The natural beauty made it a paradise that simply does not exist in the majority of the area today as construction, pollution, logging, and development have destroyed much of the natural beauty. From the stunning mountain ranges and their volcanoes to the breathtaking beaches, the native peoples were the stewards that the land deserved. For thousands of years they enjoyed the pristine lands and lived in harmony with it, and the people who lived here prior to Lewis and Clarke's arrival were varied and mostly peaceful.

California – A Real Paradise before the Greed

It is easy to feel that the native peoples who lived in the California region lived in a paradise before the initial contact with those of European descent. The California region is roughly imitated by the state lines today, stretching from the top of the state into Mexico. It had a temperate climate, making it easy for those who lived there to survive and thrive with minimal effort.

It is estimated that there were roughly 300,000 people in this region until around the middle of the 16th century. Despite being one of the smallest regions, it had one of the highest populations because of how easy it was to survive and thrive in the region. There were roughly 100 tribes who spoke an estimated 200 different dialects. Regardless of the number of different languages, they lived in relative peace, with the native peoples preferring to enjoy life than to fight over plentiful resources. According to some scholars, the diverse languages of the original California area were richer and more complex than the languages of Europe.

The people tended to live in small tribes that were based on family. They did not farm as the land provided more than enough to allow them to live freely. Despite the large number of languages spoken in the region, they traded freely with each other, sharing their arts and knowledge, as well as goods.

Spanish Invasion

Like the native peoples of the Southwestern region, the California natives had the misfortune of encountering the Spanish. With a desire for further wealth and power, the Spanish invaded the southern region of California. By 1769, the Catholic cleric Junipero Serra had created a mission in present-day San Diego. In addition to spreading the teachings of Jesus, the Spaniards often opted to enslave or murder the native peoples rather than convert them when they showed any resistance to the Spanish. By the time the Spanish terror was ended, they had exterminated entire cultures, decimating the population of these peaceful people.

Further Torment by Americans

The Americans who would steadily arrive over the next 100 years were hardly much better than the savagery of the Spanish people. The California Gold Rush whipped greedy and desperate Americans into a frenzy, and some of them quickly murdered or pressed the remaining native population off of the land they had occupied for tens of thousands of years. The American's claim that was just was illegitimate and greedy as the Spaniards who came before them. Nor were the Americans' policies any better than the Spaniards. The genocide of native peoples has been well-documented in the region because of how horrifyingly popular it was. It was something that men would brag about to others, including the local media. Men would hunt the natives to their homes, then kill everyone, including children. One such vigilante claimed that he "could not bear to kill these children with his 56-caliber Spencer rifle. 'It tore them up so bad.' So he did it with his 38-caliber Smith and Wesson revolver." This kind of psychopathic thinking was far too common among some Americans at the time.

By the time Americans began to invade the area, the population of the native peoples was less than 50,000 people. By 1900, the population had declined to only about 20,000 people. Some historians today, such as Benjamin Madley, point to the slaughter of California natives by both the Spanish and Americans as being comparable to the Holocaust and genocides in Armenia and Rwanda. It is a bloody chapter in American history that the nation largely refuses to acknowledge, hiding behind the passage of time as a weak justification. Claiming that it happened so long ago does not acknowledge the problem nor does it begin to make amends for what was done to the native peoples.

During the 20th century, Native American people began to fight through the legal systems that were supposed to uphold justice. Much like the controversial decisions in favor of the Cherokee in the 19th century (that President Andrew Jackson ignored, electing instead to forward his illegal and unethical policy of genocide and removal), the US Supreme Court ruled in favor of the native peoples in 1987. Although casinos and gambling were illegal, no rules of the US or the state of California could be applied to the Native American people. As a result, the native peoples began to improve their political and economic situations by building casinos and attracting the money of the descendants of the people who had come to California looking for easy money during the California Gold Rush.

Today, the native Californians have actually seen the greatest rise in population through all of North America. It is estimated that there are nearly 725,000 Native Americans in the region today.

The Northwest Coast – Plentiful, Peaceful, and Civilized

The native peoples of the Northwest Coast were similar to those in the Southeastern region, though they did not have to farm because of the abundance of fish, animals, berries and nuts in the region. Stretching from British Columbia to present-day northern California (the area referred to today as the Cascade region), the area was gorgeous and temperate. Not only were fish plentiful, the ocean provided other types of prey, such as seals, whales, sea otters, and shellfish. The forests and terrain were stunningly beautiful and staggeringly bountiful.

The people native to the Northwest Coast were able to establish villages with hundreds of peoples while living a lifestyle as hunters and gathers. Because of how plentiful everything was, the Native Americans of the Northwest Coast did not need to leave their homes to be successful in getting food. The migratory periods of the animals that they lived of off dove-tailed so that there was always plenty of food. Because larger mammals with thicker coats also being readily available, they were able to stay warm in the winter months and hunt without having to travel too far from home into the snow-covered Cascade Mountain range that lined the eastern side of the region.

With hundreds of people living in the villages, the people had a much more rigid social structure than those in the surrounding regions. Having a more stratified social structure made these people much more similar to the natives in Central and South America than most of the other peoples in North America. The chief of a village received the greatest recognition, and those who were related to him enjoyed more prestige within the village. Those at the top of the social structure had more possessions, including slaves, than those who were outside of the chief's social circle. The most prominent native peoples of the region include the Athapaskan Haida, Coos, Kwakiutl, Penutian Chinook, and Wakashan.

Their homes tended to be longhouses that were constructed from cedar planks. As the head of the tribe, the chief would determine who resided in which longhouse. However, if a man and his family built a longhouse alone, it would be theirs alone. When the person who owned the longhouse died, the residence was burned for fear that the owner would haunt the family if they did not move on with their lives.

The Potlatch

One of the most intriguing aspects of the complex social structure of the Northwestern natives was the Potlatch. Large, life-changing events were celebrated with a gathering of peoples, and the higher on the social ladder a person hosting the celebration was, the larger the Potlatch. The opulent celebration included a ceremonial feast. Typical reasons to have a Potlatch include the birth of a child or a wedding. The person who was hosting the ceremony would give gifts to members of the tribe as a way of demonstrating their ability to give lavishly. Land could be lent for the celebration, and then be subsequently destroyed to show just how wealthy the host was, or it could be given to others. It was meant as a way of sharing their wealth as well, giving to the people in an effort to show respect and gratitude. This tended to help build better relationships and strengthen the position of the host. The chief was always male, but those who took the position would not be guaranteed it from birth. Those who were in consideration to be chief were expected to save as much as possible, some saving for most of their lives, only to give most or all of it away as part of the Potlatch.

The Importance of Totem Poles

Few native peoples had the same outlook on totem poles as the natives of the Northwest Coast. Though they did not begin in the Northwestern Coast region, the natives loved the look and rich history that could be displayed through an intricate totem pole. Without a written language, the native peoples relied on the totem poles as a way of showing the history of a family, much like the family trees used by Europeans and their descendants. However, these were more elaborate and durable than the recordings kept by Romans and monarchies because totem poles were carved from wood and could be added to over time. They were the record of a family's history, and so were displayed very publicly for all to see. Different animals, plants, and spirits would be carved into the wood to show a new story in the family's history.

Chapter 8 – Hiawatha, Deganawida, and the Foundation for Democracies Today

Though little is known about the native peoples' history prior to the arrival of the Europeans, there are still some stories that had such a great impact on the people of the time that they are still spoken of today. One such legendary person was Hiawatha. Even people today have heard of his name, even if they don't know anything about his history or his effect on the tribes and settlers that are still felt today. He was not simply a chief who was well respected, the direction that he would lead his people resulted in the founding of the Iroquois Nation, and a few centuries later their confederation would be a primary influence for the government of the US.

He did not work alone though. Hiawatha was a peaceful man, but the vision behind the peaceful change among the five primary tribes belonged to Deganawida.

Where the Myth Starts

Prior to the founding of the Iroquois Confederacy, the people of the Northeastern Woodlands were constantly at war. The perpetual strife had taken its toll, but it seemed like an impossible feat to get the tribes to finally set aside their differences and make peace. The five tribes who were in constant war were the Cayuga, Mohawk, Oneida, Onondaga, and Seneca, and they were called the Five Nations.

It is believed that Hiawatha was born around 1525, more than 50 years before the English would make their first failed attempt at settling in the New World. Born into the Onondaga tribe, his early years were spent between what is now the Saint Lawrence River and Lake Champlain. His tribe was as war-like as the others, and it was proving to be a significant drain on the similar tribes. As they killed their own people through wars, the people who had so much in common continually weakened themselves, making them easy targets for other tribes. At some point, Hiawatha was either captured or orphaned, and the Mohawks adopted him.

Having lived among two different tribes, Hiawatha wanted peace for his people. There was so much common ground that it made no sense for them to be killing each other constantly.

The myth says that he became the chief of his tribe and had seven daughters. One of his enemies tried to woo each of them in turn. As each daughter rejected the suitor, he would kill her. Feeling completely devastated after the death of all of his daughters, the chief went into the wilds to grieve. As he traversed the wilds, he encountered the prophet Deganawida. The prophet had been unsuccessful at trying to sway people to peace because he had a speech impediment. Hiawatha was an eloquent man who was able to sway opinions and ideas, and he currently did not feel he had a purpose but he found one as a result of his meeting with Deganawida.

They returned together and began to change both the way the five tribes interacted and the way they would govern themselves.

Uniting the Tribes

Together, Hiawatha and Deganawida began to speak to the members of the other tribes. Deganawida had been the Onondaga tribe's spiritual leader, so they were willing to listen to him and Hiawatha. When Deganawida told them that he had had a vision of peace, and it was better orated by Hiawatha, the people listened. They began to share in the vision of the two men, a prophet and a wise man. It was not an easy task in front of them because peace had not been known in the region for many years.

The two men moved from one tribe to another promoting the idea of peace and trying to get the chiefs and their people to understand the importance of ending the constant fighting. After traveling to all of the tribes, they were able to get a council together to discuss their idea for "The Great Law of Peace." From that council, five primary objectives were discussed.

1. The people wanted to eliminate the perpetual wars between the Iroquois tribes.

2. They wanted to create a lasting peace that would strengthen them, creating a confederation of Iroquois.

3. The people sought to find a way to protect themselves from invasion, regardless of who the invaders were.

4. They desired expansion for their lands and power.

5. The resulting agreement would require representation and agreement in a government that all tribes abide by in the nation.

The result was the founding of the Iroquois Nation and an unwritten Constitution of Iroquois Confederacy. There were 117 Articles in the Constitution, covering a wide range of interests, concerns, and eligibility to join the Confederacy. It was fairly comprehensive, and it addressed emigration, the rights that foreign nations would have in their lands, the rules that must be followed for secession, as well as the punishment for treason. Perhaps most importantly, it stated what rights were guaranteed to the people within the nation.

Honoring the Ideas and Peace Brought through Extraordinary Efforts

The legend of Hiawatha lived on long after his death, and Americans remained in awe of his abilities based on the long-lasting effects. In 1855, Henry Wadsworth Longfellow, the famous American poet, published an epic poem about the man and the influence he had over not only his people but on the foundation of an entire nation. The epic poem is called *The Song of Hiawatha*. It should be noted that this is the American romanization of a Native American event that happened long before the English tried to settle on the continent. It did not follow the oral tradition of the people who were more familiar with the actual history, so it likely exaggerates some aspects and minimizes others. It also fails to cover how Hiawatha created an entire nation from people who previously spent much of their time in strife. The poem should be taken for what it is, the work of a poet trying to put an idea into words instead of writing an accurate history. Just as *The Iliad* and *The Odyssey* are works of fiction based on a small grain of truth, Longfellow's work only had a few parts that were accurate. Still, it is nice that some Americans understood that the histories of the native peoples were far more complex than assumed and worth romanticizing.

How the Peace of the Iroquois Confederacy Influenced Democracies Today

Most people today believe that the democracies that are spread all over the world today were founded based on the Democracy of Ancient Greece. This could be true for some democracies, but those that are based on the US idea of democracy were actually influenced primarily by the Iroquois Nation, not the Greeks. Pieces were borrowed from the Ancient Greeks, but the founding fathers had a much closer template that they used.

One of the greatest admirers of the very detailed Iroquois Constitution was Benjamin Franklin. He saw how well the nation had been able to govern itself for several hundred years, and the people were far better off than the colonials. Crime was far less common among the native peoples, and they had laws that covered actions that were a constant problem for colonials. When the War of Independence ended with the colonies breaking away from the crown, Franklin used the Constitution of Hiawatha from centuries before as the basis for the Articles of Confederation. In 1777, these articles were adopted by Congress. Today, many of those ideas are part of the fabric of the US and the way it governs.

Chapter 9 – Roanoke – The Lost Settlement

As the Spanish and Portuguese conquistadores were invading and taking what they could in South and Central America, British settlers were first starting to settle in North America. Sir Walter Raleigh initiated their first attempt, and the settlement was named Roanoke. What happened to this settlement has been a mystery for centuries. There are some theories about what happened, and there is one theory that is generally accepted as the most likely scenario for the fate of the 115 Europeans settled there. Over time, the Roanoke settlement came to be known as the Lost Colony.

The First Attempt

England watched as Spain and Portugal returned from the New World with riches far beyond anything that had been imaginable previously. The rulers of those countries were getting wealthier and gaining influence that was beyond anything that the other European countries could gain by traditional means. Of course, there were pirates and foreign governments that authorized attacks on ships returning with those riches. Still, it was not nearly as enriching as what was apparently possible by staking a claim on the lands on the new continents.

Queen Elizabeth I saw colonization as the best way to gain superiority over continental Europe. Sir Walter Raleigh was given a charter to travel to North America and establish a settlement that would start gaining England the initial foothold that it wanted.

In 1585, Raleigh founded the first European settlement in North America in the Northeastern woodland region. Joining him in this initial endeavor were other notable historical European figures, such as John White (who was named the governor of the new colony), Sir Richard Greenville, and Ralph Lane. They named the settlement Roanoke. Located on Roanoke Island off modern-day North Carolina, it was meant to be the perfect place for settlers to have a secure place to start building their new life.

It did not take long before it became very clear that the settlers were not ready for the challenges of living outside of the city. They certainly weren't prepared for what was required in the New World. They did not bring adequate food or supplies to sustain themselves for the period of time they needed to make the basics of what they needed to survive. Nor did they know how to build homes that would be able to withstand the environment. Finally, the Native Americans were not afraid to attack the people invading their lands. It did not matter to the native peoples how far the newcomers had traveled; they wanted to protect their lands from invasion.

Soon the colonists had packed up and headed home. They had learned that it would take a lot more than they had originally thought to take control over the land as the queen had wanted.

Trying Again

It took two years after the initial failure at Roanoke Island for England to try again. In 1587, more settlers returned to try to settle the area. Again, the settlement was called Roanoke, but the second attempt at settlement was different than the first attempt. During that August, 115 men, women, and children trekked across the ocean to try to build a new life. They were there, ostensibly, to help give England more power on a global scale, but most of the settlers wanted to start over in a new life. Governor White had promised them land and a say in the way the new government would be formed in the New World. This was the kind of start that the 115 people wanted.

Unfortunately, they had set off too late from Europe, and by the time they arrived at their destination, it was too late to start farming for the year. Lane had not learned any lessons with their interactions with Native Americans, and he quickly alienated them. The very people who could have helped them after their late arrival had no reason to help the settlers to survive as winter set in.

When it became obvious that the people were in dire need of new supplies, they decided that someone would need to return for those supplies. The obvious choice was to send their governor, White. He kissed his wife, daughter, and newborn granddaughter goodbye. His daughter, named Virginia Dare, was the first person of European descent born in North America, and now he would have to leave her and his wife behind. Planning to collect what was needed as quickly as possible, White returned to England to get the supplies he thought would help the settlers. He had meant to return as quickly as possible, but the timing of the return home proved to be terrible. The tensions between England and Spain had erupted into all-out war. The queen requisitioned all ships, and they were forced to work to confront the much larger Spanish Armada.

It took over two years before White was able to return to the colony. In August of 1590, he finally reached the place where he had left his family, hoping to find that things had gone better than the colonists had expected. His hopes were quickly dashed as there were no signs of anyone in the colony. No people remained in the place where he knew they should have been settled. There were only two clues as to what happened to the people who had stayed behind. The word Croatoan was carved into a wooden fence post, and the letters CRO was carved into a tree.

Croatoan Island (now called Hatteras Island) seemed to be the place where he would find those he had left behind more than two years before. However, he was unable to reach the island because of a severe storm.

Theories Abound

With only two obscure clues about what had happened to the settlement, theories began to be suggested about the fate of the people after White's departure back to England. Considering that White had been unable to travel to the Croatoan Island with a large vessel, if the colonists had attempted it in the small water vessels they had, which were primarily rafts and small boats, they would likely have drowned before reaching the island.

Since Croatoan Island was so far away (50 miles), the remaining colonists could have tried to go to the Chesapeake Bay area in their small vessels. Croatoan was also the name of the tribe that occupied the island of the same name, so it was suggested that the native people had attacked and either captured or killed the colonists.

Other theories suggested that they were wiped out by disease, although that seems to be entirely unlikely. There were few skeletons in the location where the settlement had been established, and certainly nothing like mass graves or anything that would be expected in the event of such a viral disease. There were also no homes remaining on the location where the colony had first been established.

Another theory was that the people were unprepared for the hurricanes and severe storms that are common in this part of North America. Of course, they would not have been prepared for a hurricane as these are incredibly rare in England, but it is highly unlikely that a storm would have killed more than 100 people. Also, the carvings on the tree and post showed that there had been some people who had survived. The question was what had happened to those people? Perhaps they had left some other clues, but with more than two years passing before White's return, there were no other clues that remained after all of that time.

The most obvious theory was not postured for a very long time. The native peoples were considered savage barbarians by the English. The natives had attacked the first settlement and proved to be unwilling to help the second colony when it was obviously in need. The English refused to recognize that many of their problems with the Native Americans were actually the fault of the English. They had no regard for the native people, yet expected to be accommodated when the need for help arose without giving anything back.

For more than 400 years, the fate of the second Roanoke settlement remained a mystery. Many people have dedicated a lot of time to trying to solve one of the greatest mysteries in American history, even though it happened long before the country itself existed. Theories came and went. People came up with even less likely scenarios than illness, with aliens even being suggested as the cause for the settlers' disappearance. Today, many people are beginning to believe that the obvious fate is very likely what happened.

Facing the Likely Truth – with Proof

There were many aspects of a settler's life that the English clearly did not understand, even after their initial failed attempt. One condition that no one had considered for several hundred years was first explored in 1998. Archaeologies began to study trees that were around when the settlers arrived. By studying the rings of those trees, they were able to determine that there had been a drought between 1587 and 1589. This suggested that even if the settlers had arrived early enough to plant crops, they might not have been able to have successfully grow the food necessary for more than 100 people. Given the meager supplies that they had, it is highly unlike that the settlers would have been able to survive without assistance.

Archaeologists and historians have spent years looking for any other clues about the fate of the people of the Lost Colony. Several new hints about the survivors have surfaced over the last few decades.

Several European objects were found on Hatteras Island (once called Croatoan), which is located roughly 50 miles from the initial settlement. Other objects were found 50 miles away on the mainland northwest of the settlement. Items such as sword hilts and English bowls discovered in these areas suggested that settlers moved in two different directions after it became apparent that they would not be able to survive as a colony. The problem with the finds is that they are incredibly difficult to date historically. It is not easy to determine the age of many older objects. Even if an object's age can be determined, such as a gold signet ring that had the markings of the late 17th century and was clearly a piece of jewelry worn by an English nobleman, it could have been lost at a later time. Finally, the artifacts could have been taken by Native Americans, with or without the settlers' consent. If the place was left empty, there was nothing to keep the native peoples from taking whatever they felt they could use.

It is also uncertain if they were taken away by the Native Americans, or if they peacefully assimilated into a tribe because they knew that they would not survive otherwise. It is possible that both scenarios are the case. Some may have been taken away, and those left behind may have headed west to see if any of the native peoples would take pity on them.

It is probable that the settlers who survived did join the Native Americans, and learned to live entirely different lives. The artifacts certainly suggest that this was the case. Many of the settlers had been seeking a new life, and while this may not have been what they had in mind, it was certainly new. Regardless of where they ended up, it is also clear that they integrated into the cultures where they found themselves. Even if Native Americans had taken them away as slaves, slaves had a completely different existence than what the Europeans would eventually introduce on the continent. Slaves became a part of the tribes and nations and would eventually be included in decision making, and could even marry members of the tribe. It is likely that the people of the Lost Colony assimilated so well that when Europeans tried to figure out what happened to them, they could not be found. After all, if the native peoples helped ensure their survival, it made more sense to remain with them than to rejoin more settlers who did not know how to survive in the New World. Since Europeans considered the natives to be far beneath them, it may have seemed impossible to some that civilized people would ever choose to accept what the Europeans would have considered a lesser life. Not having experienced the difficulties or been faced with death themselves, it was easy to pretend that the obvious solution was not true. This means that they very likely did not seriously look into the chance that the Europeans had fully joined the Native Americans. It would be nearly two decades before England would attempt another colony. After so many years, any surviving people from the Lost Colony would probably remember that life as a completely different life. It is unlikely that they would have wanted to start over again with more colonists who did not have the experience or knowledge that the people of the Lost Colony had acquired by assimilating with the native peoples of the continent. It is also entirely unlikely that they would have even been aware of any new attempts by England to try again.

Chapter 10 – Pocahontas – Leader, Not a Princess

One of the most legendary Native Americans wasn't even a teenager when she changed the course of history. Today, there are many myths and even a highly inaccurate Disney movie about Pocahontas. She is one of only two Native American women who are still household names today. Given that she did marry an Englishman, the US tends to romanticize her more than Sacagawea (who was a married mother when she aided Lewis and Clarke on their trip across the North American continent).

Much of what people think they know about her is based on the tendencies of Europeans and Americans to romanticize events instead of remembering them the way they were. Alterations to her story began back in the 1600s, and these myths and inaccurate recounts have been perpetuated and enhanced over the centuries.

A Quick Disclaimer

The truth of the event is not only completely uncertain, but it may also not have even happened. When the settlers arrived in Virginia, the native peoples did not have any written language. All that has come down through the ages is on the side of the settlers, and they were prone to exaggeration and coming up with stories. Truth may be stranger than fiction, but basic survival is actually pretty boring to read about. In an attempt to make their feats seem more worthy to people back in England, settlers would make up tales of events that didn't happen to show that they were the adventurers they claimed to be. There is no doubt that surviving on a new continent was incredibly difficult, particularly for people who lived in England and had little to no idea what living in nature was like or how difficult it was to create something from scratch. Since they could not understand the New World before they arrived, they knew that people back home would not understand the struggles that they went through every day. So drama was added to make their tales more harrowing, their feats more impressive, and the situations unrealistically dire.

The account told by Captain John Smith was without a doubt embellished. It is even possible that the entire thing was made up and that there was never a need for a woman to save him from execution. Since the US went on an immoral crusade against the native peoples in the years following the story's creation, and the native peoples could not record their side of the event, there is no way to verify any of the facts of the tale that Smith recounted. It is perhaps just another tale with only a few hints of facts mixed into it.

An Original Story

Whatever the motive behind Smith's telling of the tale, the legend of Pocahontas has become the original story of the United States. She is made out to be a heroine who saved not only John Smith from execution, but all of Jamestown from destruction. Without her intercession, the settlement would have failed. That is how the story has come to be told.

The location was at James Fort along the James River. The original fort has long since rotted and new homes and locations built over it because it was originally built 400 years ago. There have been re-creations of it, but some believe that the original site, or what was left of it, was only eroded away by the river. Based on maps and scientific findings, only a part of the fort was actually washed away.

John Smith became an English soldier because he didn't want to be a farmer or merchant. As a soldier, he was captured and became a slave. He escaped and returned to England where he became an adventurer.

At 27 years old, he became one of the crew of 100 men who traveled to the New World. Upon their arrival, they were attacked by the native peoples. The settlers were highly skilled in their respective fields so that they could turn a venture into a profit in a short amount of time. The plan had been for the English to trade for food instead of wasting time on agriculture, so they were not prepared to have to sustain themselves in the New World. Instead of agricultural tools, they had cheap trinkets and bits of copper that were meant to be traded for the food they needed. The men had set to work quickly trying to make a profit for the people who provided money for the trip. They did not cultivate healthy relationships with the native peoples that the plan had relied on them using to ensure their survival. The initial skirmish between the settlers and the natives did not set a positive tone, and within four months of their arrival, trading had been sporadic at best, and their relationships with the natives were far more hostile than helpful. As winter approached, it was too late to grow the food they needed. In September 1607, they were almost out of the store of food they had brought with them. Only 46 of the original 100 men who had traveled to the New World were still alive.

Hoping to find natives who would trade for the cheap items they had brought with them, Smith traveled up the river. In December of 1607, he left his craft with a native guide. They were attacked, and the natives held him captive for several weeks to a month. His captors were the Powhatan, estimated to be around 15,000 people who followed Chief Powhatan. Smith was taken to see the chief, and his admiration for what he called a savage was expressed in his writings. Despite seeing the people as savages, Smith seemed to have seen them at least as equals, and he held them in awe, unlike the settlers who would come later.

When Smith met the chief, a girl was present, and her name was Amonute. The name Pocahontas was the name she earned when she moved to her father's house. The name has a few different translations, including "playful one" and "ill-behaved child," both of which put the encounter into an entirely different light than it is seen today. No older than 12 years old when Smith was brought before her father, Pocahontas was still a child even by 17th century standards (both Native American and English). Considering the fact that Smith would not write about that encounter until 17 years later, it is easy to question not only the accuracy but the entire history that he recounted.

According to the account that he told so long after the event, Powhatan had decided to execute him. He recounted how they had placed his head on a rock, with many people touching him and forcing him into position. They readied their clubs and weapons to strike his head. Before anyone could strike, he says that Pocahontas placed her arms around his head and placed her own head on his to protect him from the execution.

It is also possible that he simply misunderstood a tradition of the Powhatan because he did not speak their language. What happened could have been part of a ceremony or other tradition. Smith himself recounted that they had him drink water and clean his hands before the event, appearing to be cordial. He even acknowledged how fierce the chief looked during the meeting, and Europeans believed the people to be savage. His assumptions about what was happening may have led to an entirely inaccurate portrayal of what actually happened. Even after hundreds of years on the same continent, Americans still fail to understand Native American customs, so this is just as likely as any other possibility. Smith did not attempt to attribute any motive to Pocahontas—that was done by others later. In England and Europe, most women were still treated as property, and many could not understand a woman doing anything for a man without there being romantic sentiment. Despite being ruled by a queen, even the English did not think women were capable of much.

It is often postulated that one of the reasons why Queen Elizabeth did not marry was because she did not want to answer to a man or lose the power she had by marrying. Had she married, her husband would have been the one in power, and she would have been expected to be just his wife— even though she was the rightful ruler. It is no wonder they could not see any other reason beyond a romantic interest, despite the fact that Pocahontas was still a child.

The Native Americans did not have the same misogynistic view of women. She would have learned much from watching her father and would have been included in negotiations and decisions by the chief. Women could become chiefs, so if she did actually act as Smith suggested, it was very likely politically driven. Since it is impossible to know if the event happened, there is little reason to speculate on it. However, since it is impossible to stop speculation, it is a good idea to try to bring up better explanations than the stale romantic interest between a child and a man about to turn 28 years old.

According to Smith's own description of Pocahontas, she was very fair. He recounted how Chief Powhatan's people said that she was a brilliant child who had a lively spirit. Everyone appeared to have high hopes for her and treated her with respect, not just because she was the chief's daughter, but because of her own merit and abilities.

Given that no one in England could refute his claims, it is possible that Pocahontas made a very good impression on him at the time. Based on his descriptions of her, particularly her appearance, saying that she was better looking than any other woman on the continent, it is possible that Smith had more of a romantic interest in her. This could have caused him to write an entirely fictitious account that showed her saving him. Also, he was trying to sell his memoirs, and adding an element of a love story would attract more attention than if it was just an adventure story.

It is also possible that his time among the natives showed him not only how they were more than just savages but taught him a much deeper appreciation for the women. Native American women were far more opinionated and respected by men than European women at the time. Because they were freer, these women would have appeared stronger, more capable, and intelligent. His own awe for the girl could have made him want to show just how amazing she was, and anything short of saving his life likely would not have impressed those back in England.

One of the reasons that the romance idea has been perpetuated over centuries is because it is incredibly flattering to the English. The same story of Pocahontas is not popular among the descendants of the Native American people, which indicates that the story was probably more fiction. However, since it was flattering to one of the earliest settlers, Americans have chosen to push the idea over the centuries. It shows that an intelligent, beautiful woman was attached to this newcomer despite all odds, much like *Romeo and Juliet*. However, given her age, this is actually a rather unsettling account of attributing attraction as the sole reason for a young girl to act in the way she did. If events did occur in the way that Smith recounted, there are many potential reasons, and attraction is not nearly so high up on the list of possibilities. He was unkempt and injured having been shot in the leg with an arrow during his capture, as well as being what would have been considered an old man for someone who was no older than 12. An old, unkempt prisoner would probably have been as unappealing to a 12-year-old in 1609 as he would be to a 12-year-old girl today.

What Is Known

Pocahontas married a warrior of her people named Kocoum. However, the marriage was likely dissolved because the English captured her around 1612 or 1613. As the settlers allied with one of the tribes that had a dubious connection to the chief, they tricked her into boarding their ship. Holding her hostage, they used her to attempt to gain the release of some of their own men from her people. When the Powhatan refused, the English kept her.

While she was in captivity, they had her convert to Christianity, whether she did so willingly or not is definitely debatable. They baptized her and renamed her Rebecca. Little else is known about the year when they kept her captive, apart from the fact that she met John Rolfe during that time. When violence erupted again in the early spring of 1614, Pocahontas was sent to talk to her father in the hopes that it would be a successful diplomatic move. During that time, she said that she would prefer to remain with her captors than return to him.

John Rolfe had become infatuated with Pocahontas. Having lost his first wife and child during the crossing to North America, it appeared he was ready to find a new wife. He asked the governor if he could marry Pocahontas, expressing a deep love for her and a desire to save her soul through a Christian marriage. The request was approved and they were wed on April 5, 1614. There is no record of how she felt about the marriage.

They lived on his farm, and two years later she had a son who was named Thomas Rolfe. The fact that she remained nearby and that her life appeared to be stable helped to build a period of peace between the settlers and the natives. Seeing an opportunity to prove that they were "taming the savages," the English decided to send Pocahontas to England, and she, her husband, and their son arrived in 1616, along with a few other natives. Naturally, they described her as a princess, though she was certainly not one, and attracted more attention and praise because of the claim. However, it also meant that she was treated well in England. She died shortly after returning home of an illness she contracted on the ship.

Until the Disney movie was released, it was actually somewhat difficult to get Native Americans from the region to discuss her because of how often she was brought up by Europeans and Americans. Though Disney's version was wildly and blatantly inaccurate (she was certainly not a buxom young woman), it actually focused on Pocahontas instead of on John Smith. This helped to revitalize the discussion as the modern-day Powhatans realized that they should be putting forth their version of the story after centuries of Smith's fiction dominating the historical records. It is difficult to know exactly how the Powhatans felt about her before the movie's release as they generally sighed and showed displeasure when asked about her. They were not inclined to discussing their side of the narrative until she was portrayed not as a woman enamored on Cook, but a strong woman in her own right who was able to choose right for reasons beyond romance. Though the movie is incredibly inaccurate, she is clearly not a pawn in it. This could have helped to make it easier to discuss her as American's way of thinking began to change about the history behind the legend.

Chapter 11 – The Real First Thanksgiving – The Myth Versus Reality

Over the years, a certain narrative has been created about what happened at the first Thanksgiving feast. The highly romanticized version of the story has the Pilgrims sitting down with an unknown Native American tribe, celebrating a peaceful coexistence with a bountiful meal. The Pilgrims were thankful for the assistance of the native peoples because they would not have survived without their kindness.

A look at actual history proves that little of the sentiment ascribed to the time is realistic. While the Pilgrims probably would not have survived without the help of the Native Americans, their gratitude directly correlated to how much they needed help. The fact that white people now reside in the area and none of the territory is occupied by the native peoples says much about how the actual settlers felt about the Native Americans.

The Rise of the Mythic "First Thanksgiving"

As one historian has pointed out, if the Pilgrims were to learn about the way Thanksgiving is celebrated today, with floats and drinking, they would be apoplectic. What is considered a family-friendly version today would not have been seen that way by the original colonists. From representing the natives as being treated as equals to the Pilgrims needing their help in order to survive, there is very little about the way it is celebrated today that the Pilgrims would not have resented.

Today, the American Thanksgiving occurs in November. If nothing else, this seems like a logical time for the holiday only because most people don't understand when harvests occur. People removed from farming and the harvesting season of the northeast think of November as the time when farmers finish reaping the benefits of the spring planting. This shows how far removed from agriculture the majority of people are.

Next is the idea that the Pilgrims either invited the Native Americans or that the Europeans were in any way managing the meal. Given that they knew little to nothing about survival in a wilderness area (they were not accustomed to what was needed for survival as they came from an area in England where they had homes that were already built and more readily available food and established fields for farming), the Pilgrims really didn't have any idea what they were doing. Without the natives, there wouldn't have been enough food for the Pilgrims to eat, let alone enough to share with others.

The images of the two groups of people, roughly evenly split, sitting at a large table with turkey as the primary food is clearly made for children, not full-grown, logical adults. Considering how ill-prepared the Pilgrims were for life in the New World, the idea that they had long tables that they used for dining is humorous. They had tables, but nothing that could have handled a feast or large meal.

One of the many pieces of propaganda perpetuated throughout the ages is that the native peoples were in awe of the "advanced technology" and skills of the English. This suggestion is also very humorous considering the Pilgrims would likely have suffered the same fate as the people of Roanoke without the kindness and pity of the native peoples.

Perhaps the saddest myth regarding the first Thanksgiving is that it established a mutual trust between the two peoples. This is far from true, and the real history should have taught the native peoples not to assist the people arriving from Europe as they were neither appreciative nor respectful, no matter how much the natives were helpful to them.

What Really Happened

To start, the Canadian Thanksgiving is probably a lot closer to when the first Thanksgiving actually happened. In the northeast, crops are harvested in either late September or early October. Typically, there is already snow on the ground by the end of November, when the US celebrates it. It's not fall anymore—it's winter and not a time for people to be eating at tables outside.

As was seen with several of the early settlements, not all of the indigenous people were accepting of the people arriving on ships. Just as you would not be happy with someone suddenly deciding that part of your yard belongs to them because they have a "divine right" to it, many natives were wary or even openly hostile to the colonists arriving. Some native peoples took pity on the ill-equipped, clearly unprepared people from England, and they did help and teach them some of the things that they needed to know. However, the idea of them celebrating like the myth is clearly inaccurate. If it was true that the Pilgrims actually had managed to amass adequate food for a feast, that was a surprise, and not something they really planned for. They would have invited the native peoples to enjoy it with them not realizing just how inadequate the amount of food was for a celebration with additional people. The Wampanoag, who were kind enough to help the Pilgrims survive, were responsible for managing the festivities and food. There were roughly twice as many of them as there were of the Pilgrims. They also brought the primary food, five large deer, as roughly 100 members of the tribe arrived for the meal.

In the absence of long tables, and certainly a shortage of the number of chairs required, it is likely that the first Thanksgiving wasn't too different to the way it is today in terms of people hanging around waiting for the food to finish cooking. They likely ate the food from the spits as it was done. Since forks were not popularly used in "civilized" Europe until the middle to end of the 17th century (they were used by the people of the Byzantine Empire and Middle East since the 11th century but were not accepted as eating utensils in Italy until centuries later, and still centuries after that in France and England), both the natives and Pilgrims ate with knives and their fingers, probably while standing.

Turkeys were probably a part of the first Thanksgiving, but the main food was the five deer that the Wampanoag brought, with duck, fish, and geese being the primary meats before the deer arrived. Also, the Pilgrims were not teetotalers, and they enjoyed beer during the meal. This alcohol would have been made from the barley that they harvested. This shows that at least the consumption of alcohol is actually an accurate tradition for Thanksgiving.

Not only did the Wampanoag not feel awed by the Pilgrims, they largely saw them as wayward children trying to act big. The people arrived in a new land with no idea how to survive. While they did have more durable clothing and superior weapons, their survival skills were comparable to that of elementary school children who do not even have enough understanding of the world to realize how little they know.

The feast was much more similar to the native peoples' Green Corn Festival and the European's traditional harvest festivals. Like today, it was mostly a secular celebration of their ability to survive in the new lands. It was only a couple of years later when the celebration took on a more religious tone as the Pilgrims suffered a serious drought that threatened to leave them starving in the winter. A significant amount of rains ended the summer drought, and they felt compelled to pray in thanks to their god for delivering them from a potentially devastating situation. Given how they had treated the natives after the first Thanksgiving, they quite possibly would have died without the rains as many of the natives were unlikely to help them by that time.

The peace between the two peoples was tentative at best. Neither side trusted the other side even after the feast. The Pilgrims saw the natives as savages (though to be fair they saw the English as being only slightly better because their religious fanaticism), and the natives did not trust the newcomers who clearly looked down on them despite being unable to survive on their own. Within a few months, the Pilgrims killed the chief of a nearby village and stuck his head on a pole outside of their settlement, leaving it there for years. It shows that there was always tensions and suspicions between the settlers and the native people. The way that Thanksgiving is portrayed today makes people feel more comfortable, but it fails to address the problems that existed back then and that continue today.

Chapter 12 – The Native American Role in the War for Independence

When people think about the American Revolution, many images appear. Some think of Paul Revere riding on horseback through the town; others picture George Washington crossing the Delaware, and still, others envision the Founding Fathers discussing how they wanted their new country to be governed. Perhaps the Boston Massacre comes to mind—an epithet that is pure propaganda because it was more of a skirmish than anything else. But what those images are missing is the role of the people who had the most to lose if they took sides.

Two Completely Different Fighting Styles

Europe had developed a very distinctive form of warfare, one that involved lining the troops upon opposing ends of the battlefield and sending them out onto the field to engage in battle. When they weren't fighting, soldiers walked in lines, and were supposed to keep step with a set rhythm. This was true even in the colonies. When the English and French fought to gain control over their "claimed" lands in the New World, they still used this method of warfare. But both sides also used native peoples to accomplish their goals. The French seemed to be more willing to take on a more "savage" approach because they wanted proof of the success of the natives who helped them in fighting the English. Requesting that the natives bring back parts of the bodies of those they killed. While there were Native

Americans who practiced scalping, the Europeans either encouraged or required it for their own purposes. Considering that Europeans would place remains out for natives to view, their practices could not be seen as more civilized than the practices that they criticized the native peoples for having.

Still, the method of fighting in Europe made sense for large portions of both the British Isles and France. They had large stretches of very open land. Following the template established by the Romans, they tried to apply logic and order to something that is inherently chaotic and illogical.

The Native American method of fighting was far more realistic both given the nature of war and heavily wooded landscape of North America. They used their environment to their advantage, hiding behind trees and using their superior hunting skills to track their enemy. Their method was to work in the shadows to gain informational superiority over their highly structured, less knowledgeable counterparts in the European military. This was the method that the colonists adapted, even when the natives did not take their side.

The End of One War...

For a people who considered themselves to be civilized, France and England seemed to be in a perpetual state of war. Now that they had their illegitimate land claims in North America, there was yet one more reason for the two nations to continue to try to sate their bloodlust on a new frontier. The drive for more power and dominance drove them to send men to their deaths over lands that did not legitimately belong to either of the two countries at war. The Christian belief of "turning the other cheek" was clearly corrupted into more of an "eye for an eye" than the pacifist teachings of the Jesus they claimed to follow.

Tensions between the British and French built during the early 18th century and finally erupted into the Great War for Empire during the 1750s and continued into the 1760s.

Up until this point, the Native Americans, who had been dying in alarming numbers because of the disease-carrying Europeans, were forced to pick sides or get caught in the middle of the fighting between two foreign powers on their lands. They had been able to prod the two countries into having petty battles and arguments, which provided a buffer for the native peoples. With the British and French loathing each other so openly, they either ignored the indigenous peoples, or they asked for the help of the natives in their fight against the other nation.

The British even created a position, Superintendent of Indian Affairs, to work with natives, primarily against the French. The British realized that they needed the help of the natives, as did the French.

No matter which side won, it was a losing war for Native Americans. The end result was that one of the two foreign powers would be forced off of the land. This would allow the remaining nation to turn its attention to the only other remaining enemy—the indigenous peoples, the only people with a legitimate claim to the land.

The British won, and the French were largely expelled from the coastal regions. The war had lasted about a decade and was very costly for England. Claiming that they had done the colonials a favor by forcing the French out of the New World, the British monarch began to enforce tighter controls on the colonials, as well as levying higher taxes. The colonials had no say in any of this, and they were outraged by the lack of representation in the government of the ruling island that was an entire ocean away from them. Resentment between the colonials and the British government grew.

This not only offered a way of keeping a foreign power warring, this time with itself, there was also hope that if the colonials won the Native Americans would have people more understanding to their cause. After all, the colonials had only gained a foothold because the Native Americans had helped them adapt to the new land. There were relationships and closer interactions between the native peoples and the invaders than between the native peoples and the people who had stayed on their island (Great Britain). However, just like some colonials sided with the British, some Native Americans also aided the crown. They saw their agreement as being with the British government, not an upstart group of people who seemed to want to keep fighting.

However, the English also claimed that they had sovereignty over the Native Americans, something that the natives clearly did not agree with. Realizing that the Native Americans understood treaties and were not nearly as war-like as the English and French, the English government continually used treaties to get what they wanted. The treaties were seen as an agreement between equals, not as the indigenous people being subservient or under the English government. Unfortunately, the colonists did not often follow those treaties and constantly infringed on the native people's land. It again looked like there were no winning sides for the native peoples to take because neither the English nor their unruly colonies could be trusted.

Then in 1774, the English gave many native peoples a further reason not to trust the English government and their ability to honor their treaties. When the French were expelled, they left Fort Pitt and the area around it. Seeing a way to support the claims stated in the Virginia charter, Lord Dunmore seized the fort, which was squarely in territory that was protected by treaties. Lord Dunmore's War was the result. Having taken land for Virginia and the crown that was part of protected land of the Delaware and the Shawnee, the two tribes naturally attacked the invading British. The much larger nation of the Iroquois soon joined to help their smaller tribes. When the English tried to keep the Iroquois from getting deeply involved, pointing out that there was a "Covenant Chain subsisting between us," the Iroquois rightfully demanded to know why that very covenant was being ignored by the British as they were ignoring older treaties. Peace was restored later that year, as well as the differences between the wronged Shawnees and Virginians. After that, the English were more careful about ensuring colonials did not encroach on the lands of the native peoples. However, there was no guarantee that the crown would continue to be successful as the colonials began to get increasingly dissatisfied with the number of laws and taxes being placed on them without having any say in the matter.

...And the Start of Another

When the War for Independence erupted, neither the English nor the colonists wanted to ask the native peoples to join them. Both sides claimed that they wanted the Native Americans to remain neutral because it was not their fight—it was another violent conflict by people who seemed to prefer war to peace. They claimed that they did not want the natives involved.

Of course, what they officially said and what they actually did was not the same.

George Washington was the first to officially bring Native Americans into the war when he recruited a few native people from the northeastern region to be gunmen. This happened in the winter of 1774–1775. When the British found out about Washington's inclusion of natives in 1775, they used that action as a justification for drawing a much larger group of native peoples to their side. The British commander told the superintendent of Indian Affairs in the southeastern region that they were to start involving the Native Americans as soon as there was an opportunity to do so. By the summer of that same year, the colonials had done something similar, and it largely became a race to see which side could convince the Native Americans to trust and help them in a fight that they themselves had said the natives should not be drawn into.

By the summer of 1776, both sides were trying to gain the trust of and an alliance with the most powerful northeastern nations, the Iroquois. Both sides tried to offer the natives what they thought the Native Americans desired. In a message from Vermont colonial Ethan Allen, he wanted the Iroquois to:

> Stand all along close Together Rank and file and my men fight so as Indians Do I want your Warriors to Join with me and my Warriors like Brothers and Ambush the Regulars, if you will I will Give you Money Blankets Tomahawks Knives and Paint and the Like... (The war occurred before the standardization of spelling and punctuation.)

Around the same time, the British were offering the natives "to feast on a Bostonian and drink his Blood." Understanding that the Iroquois were not cannibals, the British offered a roasted ox and wine instead of the body and blood of a Bostonian.

Initially, the Iroquois found both sides to be uninspired. As one of the Seneca warriors succinctly put it,

> We have no lived in Peace with them a long time and we resolve to continue to do so as long as we can – when they hurt us it is time enough to strike them. It is true they have encroach'd on our Lands, but of this we shall speak to them. If you are so strong Brother, and they but as a weak Boy, why ask our assistance. It is true I am tall and strong but I will reserve my strength to strike those who injure me. If you have so great plenty of Warriors, Powder, Lead and Goods, and they are so few and little of either, be strong and make good use of them You say their Powder is rotten – We have found it good. You say they are all mad, foolish, wicked, and deceitful – I say you are so and they are wise for you want us to destroy ourselves

in your War and they advise us to live in Peace. Their
advice we intend to follow.

This response could have been given to both sides as neither side
would know that the other approached the Iroquois if the Iroquois
did not join in the war. The Native Americans wanted the two
warring parties to stick to their principles. Both sides recognized that
the natives had no place in the war, yet they were both trying to win
the native peoples over to their side. It was quite obvious that both
sides were deceitful, which was one more reason not to aid either
side.

Unfortunately, there were divisions within the Iroquois Nation, and
they were finally dragged into the War for Independence after a
Mohawk returned from England, having been treated well. He
convinced four of the six nations to join the crown as he believed
that the crown would honor the Native Americans more than the
colonials. The two nations that did not want to join the war ended up
fighting on the side of the colonials at the Battle of Oriskany, and the
peoples of the Iroquois Nation ended up killing each other in a war
that they should not have joined. They suffered heavy losses of their
warriors during the battle in 1777.

The English pressed down from Canada, and a young lady was
killed. The colonials used propaganda from this to say that the
British were turning the savages against them and that the savages
were now killing indiscriminately—something that Americans were
much more inclined to do both during the War of Independence and
throughout their dishonorable treatment of native peoples. For
example, when Washington drove back the British, he and his men
took a scorched earth approach, completely destroying native lands
that they should not have been on in the first place. When the
county's first president negotiated with the leader of the Seneca
people in 1790, the leader made a point of pointing out America's
predilection for committing the crimes that they claimed were
savage. At the meeting, he told Washington, "When your army
entered the country of the Six Nations we called you Town

Destroyer; and to this day when that name is heard our women look behind them and turn pale, and our children cling close to the necks of their mothers."

However, it was the Native Americans in the southern regions who had substantially more power compared to those in the northern region. It is estimated that there were roughly 14,000 warriors between the major nations in the region, and getting these warriors to join one side would clearly provide an advantage to whichever side could persuade them. The Native Americans in the southern areas had similar treaties in place as those with the British in the north, and they were equally (and justifiably) angered by the continued encroachment on their lands and the breach of those treaties. Again, both sides tried to persuade the Native Americans (particularly the Cherokee whose land was most often encroached upon) not to join for either side.

British soldiers, including some Native Americans, from the northeastern region traveled to the southeastern region and finally persuaded the indigenous people of the area to join against the colonists. When the Cherokees were persuaded to fight against the upstarts, the future Americans' response was as cruel as when the Cherokee attacked settlers who illegally encroached on their land. Like the Iroquois though, the Cherokee had known what was to happen and they withdrew so that few of them were killed by the colonists.

The problem with the future Americans claiming that the native people were in the wrong is that they, the colonists, were the ones who were ignoring the treaties and stealing the native peoples' lands. There was far more reason for the Iroquois and Cherokee to side with the crown that seemed willing to try to keep the colonists in check. Many of these future Americans showed little to no interest in showing any restraint when it came to stealing land from the native peoples.

Many Native Americans and tribes sided with the colonies. They worked with the future Americans, particularly along the coast. For those who were no longer worried about settler encroachment, joining the colonists was the better option. To those natives, the war was personal. They agreed with the colonists that the British were in the wrong and took up arms to fight alongside the colonials as they had lived side-by-side with them for more than 150 years.

Of course, Americans want to paint the natives as being in the wrong, but the natives always fought for their way of life, which one cannot fault them for doing. Iroquois fought against their own because of how divisive the problem was. Yet this was almost completely glossed over, and the natives who sided with the colonists were not treated any better than those who sided with the British.

When it was clear that the British would lose, some nations, such as the Cherokee, began to broker peace with the future Americans. Some nations chose to continue to fight with the British and then abandoned their lands when the British left instead of sharing it with their enemies. During peace negotiations between the new country and England, nothing was said of the Native Americans. This blatant disregard for the people who had aided the British outraged a number of native nations because it was seen as a way of selling them out, despite having assisted the British in the war. In truth, it didn't matter what was in the agreement; the Americans did not feel bound by anything the British (or Spanish who had aided them and joined in the peace negotiations) said.

Had the Native Americans sided with the colonies (as some did), it would not have benefited the native peoples. It was always going to be a losing war for the Native Americans because neither side respected them as equals. Perhaps if the English crown had won, the native peoples would have suffered a similar fate to the actual Indians in Asia, with an uprising eventually forcing the British out of India. For the native peoples, there was no way to win because the new nation believed that they had a right to everything they could see, as the bloody genocide of the next 100 years would prove.

Chapter 13 – Sacagawea – The Woman Behind the Legend

While Pocahontas was viewed as being the person who saved John Smith, and by extension the survivors of Jamestown, Sacagawea is viewed as the woman who successfully guided Lewis and Clark across the Louisiana Purchase. She was not the only person to take them west, but she is generally given credit for ensuring that the trip was successful. Truly an amazing woman, she traveled more than halfway across North America with her infant son. However, she was more than just a guide to the Americans wanting to explore the new lands that had been made available to them.

The Early Life of an American Legend

One of the reasons why Sacagawea was the ideal guide was because of her early life. She was the daughter of a Shoshone chief, but she was abducted when she was only 12 or 13 years old. The Hidatsa attacked her tribe in 1800, and they took several girls from their home. It was likely that Sacagawea was specifically targeted as retribution for an earlier attack that the Shoshone had carried out against the Hidatsa. She was forced to be the second wife of Toussaint Charbonneau. He was a French-Canadian fur trader who lived with the Hidatsa in North Dakota. Because Charbonneau had made Sacagawea his wife, she would gain a lot of the necessary skills that would make her an asset for the Lewis and Clark Expedition four years later.

A New Mother and Invaluable Interpreter

Meriwether Lewis and William Clark knew that they were going to need both a guide and an interpreter to trek from the edge of the settled US to the other side of the continent. Two men, Charbonneau and Rene Jusseaume, were hired to serve as the translators for the trip. Charbonneau had brought his wives with him, and at the time Sacagawea was pregnant. The 17-year-old was not meant to play a significant role as her husband was supposed to be the one working to translate when speaking with the Hidatsa (Jusseaume was to work as the Mandan translator).

In February 1805, Sacagawea gave birth to her first son, and he was named after Charbonneau's father—Jean Baptiste. Jusseaume appears to have assisted her during the childbirth. Lewis appeared to have taken an interest in the birth but more out of mere curiosity. Two months later, the group set out, with Sacagawea carrying her infant son as she accompanied her husband and the men on the long trip. The other wives of the two translators did not join in the journey.

Lewis and Clark both recorded information about the trip, and from that, we know a lot of what happened. The increasing amount of text that they dedicated to Sacagawea proved that they learned to appreciate her presence on the trip. She was level-headed, knowledgeable, and would do work that most people didn't even realize needed to be done.

Within two days of leaving their fort, Sacagawea had begun to impart vital knowledge to the men about the foods that were available from the lands that they were traveling through. Although they appeared to not even know her name, they were impressed by how she was able to go out and find ample food to help them supplement their supplies. The details were included in the notes and journals of the two men, ensuring that history was able to pore over the beginning of one of the most notable events in the country's history.

One notable change in how they viewed the only woman in the party occurred May 15th. One of their boats upset, and Charbonneau seemed to panic. Pierre Cruzatte was the one credited with saving the supplies, but Lewis added that it was Sacagawea who had saved many of the supplies, most notably the lighter things that had been taken over the side of the craft. On May 19, they named one of the rivers they encountered after her; their awe of Sacagawea continually growing as she calmly and quickly tended to things without pretense or desire for acknowledgment.

Over time, Clark appeared to have developed a friendship with the woman who was strong enough to join them despite the fact that she had recently had her first child. He seemed to have become somewhat protective of her as well over the course of the journey. Both of the men shared the tipi (teepee) with the Charbonneaus, so they had both developed a better acquaintance with her, and she became more frequently mentioned and admired in Clark's journals. Both men appeared to have developed a certain awe of her for different reasons. Lewis greatly admired how well she could handle herself when difficult situations arose, and he seemed to take over being protective of her when Clark became ill later in the trip.

Clark acted as her primary caregiver when Sacagawea fell when they reached the Falls in Missouri. After 10 days, Lewis reported that she had returned to a more normal state and was "walking about and fishing," as well as collecting roots for the expedition to eat.

A flash flood occurred on June 29th. The Charbonneaus and Clark were in the tent at the time that the heavy rains started, but it quickly escalated into a flash flood that made the tent a trap. The husband appeared to freeze as Clark assisted in getting Sacagawea and her son out of the ravine. She had only recently recovered from the earlier incident, and Clark feared that the flood would have an adverse effect on her recovery, as well as being a threat to the infant. He immediately sent men to get clothing for her so that she could be warmed and the baby tended.

The journals also show that Sacagawea was not the guide that people often think she was. She would recognize landmarks as they crossed the various areas, but Sacagawea was not familiar enough with the region to act as a guide. It had been six years since she had been in the area and had been a child at the time. Her memories were accurate, and she was able to provide help in navigating without being able to act as a guide.

After they had been trekking for four months, they encountered the Shoshone and approached them, hoping to get some horses to ease the difficulty of their travels. The person that they encountered was Sacagawea's older brother, who was now the chief. This was clearly an opportunity for her to finally return to her people, but she chose to remain with the men journeying west. However, it was the fact that they encountered her family that convinced the Shoshone to provide aid for the expedition. Because they were able to acquire horses, the group was able to cross the intimidating Rocky Mountains with much more ease.

When the group successfully reached present-day Astoria, Oregon, Sacagawea insisted that they continue until they reached the Pacific Ocean. One of the natives in the region had told them that a whale had been beached not too far away, and she was curious to see what would have seemed like a mythical creature. Lewis wrote of how adamant she was:

> [She] was very impo[r]tunate to be permitted to go, and was therefore indulged; she observed that she had traveled a long way with us to see the great waters, and that now that monstrous fish was also to be seen, she thought it very hard she could not be permitted to see either.

The fact that they were willing to indulge her interest shows that they had gained a lot of respect for her and did not want to deny her seeing something that was new to her after she had aided them in crossing vast stretches of land that were new to them. She was also allowed to vote on where they would build a fort for the winter. Given that she was not only a prisoner and forced wife of Charbonneau but also a woman shows just how well-respected Sacagawea came to be after everything she had done for Lewis and Clark.

Disappearing into History

The family of three had joined the expedition for an estimated 16 months, out of a total of 28. When they were returning from the Pacific Ocean, the family left the adventurers near a Hidatsa village along the Missouri River. Very little is known of their life after that, save for a few points where they encountered Clark again. During his time with the family, Clark had developed a fondness for the infant who had traveled with them, and he asked Charbonneau to settle with his family in or near St. Louis. Charbonneau declined the invitation but did leave his son behind for Clark to tend and educate.

It is unknown what became of Sacagawea. She may have joined her husband as he visited one of their traveling companions, or she may not have joined him. Even the story of her death is not known. It is said that she lived with her husband along the upper Missouri River where she died in 1812 during an outbreak of the "putrid fever." Others believe that she returned to the Shoshone after having found her brother, and they say that she died in 1884. Sacagawea was thrust into a spotlight of history, probably never realizing just how much she had done for the country. It is unknown what she thought of her traveling companions or even her husband. Just as she left the expedition when she was no longer required, Sacagawea stepped out of the spotlight and faded into the background like a mythological figure. It is highly unlikely that she ever knew just how huge her influence was or how much of an impression she had left on the men who had seen her acting in every capacity that they could not.

Chapter 14 – The Seminole Wars

The Seminoles were a very different people than most of the Native Americans who lived along the east coast. Based on recent finds, the people have resided in Florida for over 14,000 years, giving them an extensive history that is unimaginable to Americans whose country is less than 300 years old. The first Europeans to encounter the tribes that became known as the Seminole Nation were the Spanish, who had already established genocide as their chosen method for dealing with the people of North and South America who did not want the Spanish on their lands. The Seminoles are generally thought of as being more hostile than other Native American tribes along the eastern coast of North America, but it is possible that this incredibly horrible first impression of Europeans made the people extremely wary of any Europeans. They were understandably defensive of the place where they had lived for literally thousands of years.

The Spanish Lose Florida Again

Spain had limited involvement in the American Revolution. As an ally of France, they assisted and helped the colonists fight against England. As they had laid claim to Florida, they assisted the future Americans from the south. When the treaty was drawn up to end the conflict known as the War for Independence, the Spanish kept Florida.

The problem was that Florida was a highly desirable property, and the Americans were far more interested in taking it from the Spanish than in being grateful for the assistance that the Spanish had provided during the American Revolution. Spain recognized the danger with this new variable of a country just north of their lands, and they encouraged settlement along the shared boundary. People from Spain and the new country were encouraged to settle, which was a mistake that the Mexicans did not learn from when they invited Americans to help them settle Texas. However, after more than a century of learning that the Seminole could not be removed as easily as the native peoples of other regions, the Spanish seemed to have established a slightly better relationship with them. Perhaps the Spanish felt a sense of respect for the Seminoles as by this point the Spanish encouraged the natives to establish farms and settlements along the border. It is also likely that they saw the Seminole as being a barrier to dissuade Americans from trying to take Florida. As if to irk the Americans, the Spanish refused to return escaped slaves who reached their lands, and they were absorbed into the growth of Florida and often worked alongside the Seminole who saw them as being in a similar situation as themselves and accepted them into their tribe.

England had ruled Florida for a time, prior to the War for Independence. During that time, they had encouraged the Seminoles to fight back against colonists who continued to push into the Seminole territory. By the time Spain regained control of Florida, the Seminole already had established a very combative relationship with the new country.

Later, under President Andrew Jackson, the US committed some of the greatest atrocities in the nation's history. During this time, Jackson was merely an ill-tempered member of the military, but it showed just how cruel and savage the man was long before the people elected him to the presidency. Disregarding the fact that Spain had helped the country to beat the British, Americans continued to invade Florida, under the claim that they were trying to get their slaves back. While some were trying to find their slaves, the fact that they didn't leave Florida proved that this was nothing more than an excuse for aggression. The actual goal was to steal the land from Spain.

In 1821, America was finally successful in driving the people who had been their allies during the country's founding from the lands that the Spanish had held before most of the colonies existed. Of course, the natives were the only ones with a legitimate claim, but based on the limited view that only Europeans and the people who followed the European god had a right to the land, the Americans had just proved that even that was a lie. They would always have an excuse to steal lands and potential resources from enemies and allies alike.

What followed was a series of wars with the Seminoles who did not recognize the US as the new owner of their lands.

The Resettlement Effort

Jackson's policies based on Manifest Destiny resulted in some of the nation's most backward and barbaric policies. Claiming Manifest Destiny, he had the US military start removing native peoples from lands where they had lived for tens of thousands of years because he only wanted white Americans to prosper on those lands. Following what Americans call the Creek War (1813 to 1814), the violent clash with the Maskoki tribes of Alabama resulted in a treaty, which the US immediately broke. When the country began to drive the Maskoki off of their own lands, many fled to Florida instead of going west as the US was trying to force them to do. Many of the Maskoki who fled were warriors who, like the Seminole, now had adequate incentive to loath and fight the US.

Having successfully fought off the Spanish for the entirety of their occupation in Florida, the Seminole considered themselves a free people. When the US tried to force them off of their lands, as the country was attempting with all natives (regardless of treaties, alliances, and, as the Cherokee later proved, against the rulings of the US Supreme Court), the Seminoles resisted. Jackson had miscalculated in his attempt to solve what he called the "Indian Problem"; the countries that traded with the US were very much opposed to his clearly immoral and barbaric practices. As a result of the international world condemning his actions, Jackson felt justified any killing of those who opposed his policies. This included two Englishmen that Jackson suspected of inciting the native peoples to fight—something that the Seminole clearly did not need any outside incentive to do. This period is known as the First Seminole War because clashes occurred frequently, and Florida was constantly erupting into bloody battles. The first war lasted from 1814 to 1818.

In a misguided and ill-thought-out attempt to gain Florida through one of their fake treaties, the US tried to persuade the growing number of native peoples in Florida to leave (the Maskoki were only one of many tribes and nations who opted to flee to Florida instead of going west). They tried to convince the people to sell their cattle and return slaves, two things that clearly would weaken the natives, which they weren't willing to do.

By 1830, Jackson had unfortunately been voted into the powerful position of President of the US where he was very abusive of his powers. Even when people within the US decried his cruelty toward natives, particularly those who lived near Native Americans and valued the long-established partnership, he ignored them. Bent on forcing the native peoples to resettle in regions where he didn't think there were adequate resources, Jackson started taking on the more difficult native peoples, most notably the Cherokee and Seminole Nations. The Cherokee chose to fight through the US court systems, a move that he had not anticipated. Since the US courts found in favor of the Cherokees, Jackson decided to ignore that particular branch of the US government and continued with his now illegal actions. The actions were illegal as he was now acting against the law of the land and acting more as a dictator than as a president. As a side note, it was a member of the Cherokee who saved Jackson's life during an earlier battle, but he never showed any sign of gratitude for that action. The end result of Jackson's racism against the

Cherokee who had literally fought alongside him and sought a peaceful resolution was the Trail of Tears.

However, the Seminole did not know the court systems as well as the Cherokee, having spent decades fighting the US instead of working alongside them. Their complete lack of trust for the US government that seemed to only make treaties to break them proved to be the more successful path. Although the fighting did not stop after 1818, the advances of the now President Jackson into Seminole territory began a much larger stint of violence. Beginning in 1835, the fighting intensified and is called the Second Seminole War.

As the Spanish had found before them, the US realized that the Seminole were not nearly as easy to remove as the other natives the US had pushed off of their lands. For the next seven years, Jackson would spend roughly $40,000,000 in an attempt to kick the native peoples off of their lands. While the other Native American removals required only the use of the US army to execute the heinous policy, Jackson had to send in the US army, navy, and marine corps in an attempt to remove the Seminole.

Also like the Spanish, the US failed. A third Seminole War was the only one where the US was able to claim a level of success. The primary leader of the Seminole Nation agreed to leave, and many of his people went with him to the new, largely inhospitable lands.

Many Seminole died, and others were forced onto ships and taken up the Mississippi River for relocation. Those who were forced to the new lands ended up in new battles with the other displaced natives because there were not adequate resources for everyone on the barren plots of land that the US had designated for them.

The Reality of the Seminole Wars

Clearly the US had underestimated the Seminole Nation, though, because they could not completely remove all of the natives. Small pockets of tribes had escaped the barbaric treatment at the hands of the US military, but a much larger number of Seminole remained in their ancestral lands.

The war against the Seminole began before the attempt to remove the Cherokee and lasted long after the Trail of Tears ended. Spanning more than two decades, it cost many lives. Many notable US military figures were pulled into the war, and they had a few takeaways from the war with the Seminole. Today, US soldiers still use the guerrilla warfare that the Seminole had mastered and used against the US with great efficiency. Other tribes fought in similar methods, but none were nearly as effective, perhaps because the Seminole had hundreds of years to master guerilla tactics against the Spanish. The US military still teaches the tactics used by the Seminole against them. Unfortunately, they didn't really learn how to do it well as they would lose to the same tactics roughly 100 years later when the US entered another illegal war against the Vietnamese.

Today, roughly 3,500 Seminole still live on their lands in Florida. Some descended from the people who never left; others are descended from people who made their way back to Florida while the US engaged in illegal wars with other native peoples further west.

Chapter 15 – Sitting Bull – Fighting Despite All Odds

The man who is called Sitting Bull by Americans has become a legendary figure in both Native American and American traditions. While Americans do know a little bit about him today, they tend to see him as a positive figure who wanted only to do what was right for his people. Distancing themselves from the fact that it was the American government that killed the legendary leader of a Lakota tribe, Americans seldom dig too deep into his history. However, they do view him as a good leader and feel that what happened was not right.

Native Americans have a decidedly different perspective of the man, particularly his descendants. He is one of the few native peoples whose name is taught in American schools, although the history is somewhat distorted. This chapter looks at the man as he is remembered by the indigenous peoples, going much further back in history than the clashes between Native Americans in the west and the cruel and obviously illegal policies of the American government at the time.

Early Life

Born near the Yellowstone River near the today's town of Miles City, Montana, the infant was originally named Jumping Badger. He belonged to the Sioux and was a Hunkpapa Sioux. Little has been passed down in the Sioux oral tradition about his childhood.

Considered slow because of his calm nature, he strove to prove he was more than what people thought of him. At just 10 years old, Jumping Badger killed a buffalo, and at 14 he joined the Lakota tribe's warriors in what was a raid against the rival Crow to steal horses.

During this raid, Jumping Badger completed his counting coup against the Crow. This meant that he won recognition from his people through courage during a raid. To celebrate his becoming a man, a feast was thrown in Jumping Badger's honor, and his father gave him a new name, Tatanka Iyotake, or "Buffalo Bull Sits Down." Now considered a man and an official warrior, the young man was given a horse, a shield, and an eagle's feather to wear.

A Shift to Leadership

By the time he was 25 years old, Sitting Bull had become the leader of a renowned group called the Strong Heart Warrior society. He had gained a reputation that caused even his enemies to hold him in awe; so effective was his leadership that his warriors could strike fear in the hearts of others by shouting "We are Sitting Bull's boys" as they charged into battle.

However, he was not just an impressive warrior. Sitting Bull was a spiritual leader who could inspire others to follow him. His visions helped to press his followers into battle and to ease the concern of those left behind to worry. When the US government tried to force Sitting Bull and his people to follow the Fort Laramie Treaty that had been signed by Red Cloud of the Oglala Lakota, he refused.

In 1874, General George Armstrong Custer invaded one of the Sioux's sacred places, the Black Hills. Gold had been found near the area, and Custer and the prospectors ignored the treaty that said they would not enter the Sioux land, as stated by the Fort Laramie Treaty. Sitting Bull was able to rally warriors from both the Lakota and the Cheyenne to fight back against the attackers. Following the defeat of Custer in a skirmish, the US demanded that all hunting bands report to their agencies at the established reservations. They were trying to protect the prospectors illegally entering Sioux land by keeping track of the warriors. This was the final straw for Sitting Bull and his followers.

The Legend, His Actions, and the Aid of Crazy Horse

In June 1876, Sitting Bull had helped to assemble between 12,000 and 15,000 warriors. They set up at the Little Bighorn River. As a spiritual leader, he also made sure that they completed ceremonies. One of the most important ceremonies was the Sun Dance Ceremony, and Sitting Bull participated in the dance for 36 hours. During that time, he experienced a vision of the result, and he relayed that he had seen that they would be victorious. The vision appeared to be coming true when, on the 17th of June, they joined in battle against General George Crook. He and his men retreated from the battlefield in what would later be called the Battle of the Rosebud.

Crazy Horse was another Lakota Sioux chief. His history somewhat paralleled Sitting Bull's (he killed a buffalo at 12 years old). After witnessing the brutal killing of a Sioux (who was trying to mediate an argument) by a soldier, he joined the fight against the US military. He became a chief at 24 years of age and refused to resettle after the Fort Laramie Treaty. Crazy Horse and his followers ignored the requirement to report to the US government following the illegal activities of prospectors entering their lands. The movements and tactics of his men were instrumental in helping defeat Crook the week before.

Eight days after the defeat of Crook, General Custer initiated an attack on Sitting Bull and his warriors, opting to strike them while the warriors were on their own territory. Following the defeat of Crook, Crazy Horse and his warriors joined Sitting Bull. They coordinated their movements. As Sitting Bull attacked Custer from the front, Crazy Horse and his warriors joined from the north and west, and Chief Gall attacked from the south and east.

The battle did not last 30 minutes and resulted in the complete annihilation of Custer, two of his brothers, one of his nephews, his brother-in-law, and all of the men under him. It is estimated that including their scouts a total of 268 US soldiers died at the battle. There were 55 who were injured, but alive, when it ended. It was clear that Custer had vastly over-estimated his abilities and underestimated how many natives he was facing. He also failed to account for how angry the Native Americans were after his illegal entry into their lands and his attempt to kill them on their own lands.

Following the victory, Sitting Bull felt obligated to point out what should have been obvious, "Let no man say that this was a massacre. They came to kill us and killed themselves." Custer had vastly overestimated his own abilities and those of the men he was to fight. Still, Sitting Bull knew that the loss of American troops would be met with retaliation, despite the fact that the soldiers had been the initial aggressors.

Both chiefs would continue to keep their people free. Knowing that the US government would never honor their agreements and would respond to the justified killing of Custer and his men, the chiefs took their people in different directions.

Crazy Horse returned with his people to Rosebud River. They were eventually defeated, and he surrendered in 1877. As part of the surrender, the US promised him a new reservation, which was another lie. Crazy Horse ended up taking his sick wife off of the reservation where they had been sent after the surrender in an attempt to get her the care she needed from her people who lived 40 miles away from the reservation. Since he had not gained permission first, Crazy Horse was taken into custody. When it became obvious that they planned to place him in the stockade, he began to fight back. A soldier ran him through with a bayonet, and he died before the next morning.

Sitting Bull faired only slightly better.

Escape to Canada, A Return, and His Final Years

Sitting Bull knew that the US government would never honor their word or treaties, and they were now after him and his people following the loss of an over-confident Custer. In an attempt to keep his people free, Sitting Bull led them to Canada where they were able to remain for four years without the constant threat from the US government. However, they could not stay, and they ended up surrendering to the US and returned to areas closer to their ancestral lands. Surrendering to the US in 1881, Sitting Bull now only had 44 men and 143 women and children left under his care. He was held as a prisoner for two years.

By this point, Sitting Bull had become a famous (or perhaps infamous) name, and Americans found themselves more interested in learning about him and seeing this fierce warrior as someone who had fought so bravely against what were considered to be impossible odds. Although he had become a successful farmer on the Standing Rock Reservation where he and his people had settled after their surrender, he joined Buffalo Bill Cody's Wild West Show. Between 1885 and 1886, Sitting Bull traveled with the show.

In 1886, Sitting Bull returned to his people. The Ghost Dance Movement was growing and the US government failed to understand its point. Fearing that such a fearsome leader would persuade his people to act against the US government, they sent soldiers to arrest Sitting Bull without any grounds. There was a struggle during the arrest, and Sitting Bull was shot multiple times. He died from the wounds and was buried near Fort Yates. His people exhumes his remains in 1953 and returned his body near to the place where he was born.

Unfortunately, this was an ill omen preceding something much worse two weeks later at Wounded Knee.

Chapter 16 – Wounded Knee – A Real American Tragedy

One of the most famous quotes Winston Churchill ever uttered was that "History is written by the victors." When looking back over the history of all countries, this is an incredibly important point to remember. The colonies won the American Revolution, and so it has come to be considered an inevitable event, if not a completely justified one (it really depends on where you live as to whether you think it was a good thing). The Allies won World War II. And the Romans conquered most of the known world (to those in that part of the known world). While the end results are debated, the fine details are very seldom debated. People tend to believe the terrible things said about those who lost, even when there is no evidence of the horrors being described by the victors. Some atrocities are undeniable, such as the Holocaust. But other historic recitals are far less believable, such as the guilt of the people killed during the Salem Witch Trials.

Propaganda has always played a crucial role in turning tides and swaying opinion, and in few places is that more pronounced than in the wholesale slaughter of the native peoples in both North and South America. When some of the people of European descent could not get what they wanted from the Native Americans, they would demonize or dehumanize them so that the American people would clamor for government intervention. This was certainly true for the Trail of Tears, because the people who lived near the Cherokee

Nation knew that the way President Jackson and the government portrayed the native peoples was a complete lie. Nor is that the only instance of an infamous theft by the American government against the Native Americans. Not all Americans bought into the lie either. Many tried to stand and fight for and with the Native Americans. However, for many Americans, it was not a problem that specifically affected them, so while they disagreed with the policy, they focused on the problems that directly affected their lives instead of engaging.

Perhaps one of the most well-known, but often misrepresented, events was the "Battle" of Wounded Knee.

Rise of the Ghost Dance

By the late 19th century, Native Americans were well aware of the lies and cruelty of the American people and their government. The Sioux people had already been relegated to a reservation, and Sitting Bull was their chief during the end of the 19th century. Like many humans throughout history, they thought that their defeat was an indication of spiritual failure. Believing their people had lost their way by becoming more integrated with Americans, the oppressed people began to return to their traditions.

The Ghost Dance was a spiritual movement that was begun by Wovoka, a Paiute mystic. The Ghost Dance was meant to give hope to the Western Native Americans that they could return to the abundance of the past, before Europeans had invaded, stolen their lands and resources, and forced them to live on small, inhospitable patches of land that the Americans had not yet found any value in. Through dance and prayer, they would find justice against those who had wronged them. It was in part a way of repenting from turning from their original ways. When the Sioux abandoned their traditions, their gods had caused them to suffer and be forced onto the reservation. The Ghost Dance itself was a sign that they were rejecting the American ways and returning to the old ways. Other native peoples learned of the movement, and it spread across many of the reservations.

Dancing has always been an important part of Native American life, both as a way of expression and spirituality, but many Americans decided that it was meant as a threat. They associated it with war, despite the fact that Europeans and Americans had their own dances and really should have known better than to attribute sinister motives to dancing.

The Ghost Dance was seen as particularly threatening, and General Nelson Miles warned the native peoples that they were to stop their Ghost Dance activities. To support his warning, 7,000 troops were deployed to monitor and control the Lakota.

The Events at Wounded Knee

The American government felt threatened by the movement, with many believing that it was a sign that the Native Americans were planning something. In December 1890, members of the US military arrived to arrest Chief Spotted Elk at Wounded Knee. The chief of a group of Miniconjou Lakota Sioux, he and roughly 350 of his people were camped at Wounded Knee Creek. The soldiers' orders were to arrest the chief and disarm his people. Given the recent murder of Chief Sitting Bull during his arrest, the Native Americans were understandably uncomfortable with the presence of the US military. However, the people were not hardened warriors—many of them were women and children as this was their makeshift camp.

Following the murder of the Sitting Bull, Chief Spotted Elk had decided to move his people to a location that would be safer. They had set up a temporary place at Pine Ridge Agency. Hearing about the movements of the people and their Ghost Dance activities, General Nelson Miles decided that the military needed to act. He sent major Samuel Whiteside and the Seventh Cavalry to Wounded Knee with the expressed direction to arrest the chief and some of his followers. On a cold, late December day in 1890, the Seventh Cavalry reached Chief Spotted Elk's camp. As the men were taking the weapons from the native peoples, a gunshot rang out.

The tension erupted, and the men who had peacefully surrendered their guns were now trying to retake them from the US military to use to defend themselves, the women, and children who were only looking for a safe haven. The soldiers immediately turned the guns on the natives and began to shoot. An early version of the machine gun had been placed on the top of the hill, and it began to shoot into the tepees and natives indiscriminately. The natives who fled to escape the gunfire from the soldiers were mowed down by the machine gun.

When the Seventh Cavalry finally stopped shooting, between 150 and 250 of the Lakota lay dead in the snow: men, women, children, and Chief Spotted Elk. Of the Cavalrymen, 20 were dead.

Rebranding the Battle Based on Facts

Following the slaughter of many innocent native people, the US falsely branded the events as the "Battle of Wounded Knee." However, this description is not backed by the facts of what happened. All of the men of the Seventh Cavalry were military personnel who were armed. They faced more than 300 Lakota, many of whom were civilians who were simply trying to find a safe place to live following further betrayals by the US against other natives. They were willingly surrendering their arms.

The debate has raged in recent years about how to classify what happened. There are still some who believe that what happened was an incredibly tragic event. Even they no longer call it a battle because it clearly was not a war or a planned event. The Lakota had not wanted any interaction with the military. It had been the US military who had forced the interaction, and the native peoples were acquiescing in the hopes of avoiding more bloodshed. The shot that rang outset the terrible events in motion, and there is some understanding of how the US troops would have been scared when they were clearly outnumbered. The problem is that they did not have any qualms with firing into the Lakota, killing people who were clearly no threat. Calling the event a battle clearly was meant to justify the actions that were unjustifiable. It was nothing more than propaganda, and for more than 100 years, many people believed that it had been much more of a struggle between the natives and the cavalry than it really was. Americans thought that the troops had been brave in the face of a bloodthirsty group of natives. The actual facts, including that many of the people killed were women and children, were largely kept from the public because it would certainly prove the fallacy of the narrative the government wanted to push. Interestingly enough, the news on what happened was reported on in Europe, and the media there had a completely different take— they were united and "almost uniformly treated [the events at Wounded Knee] as a bloodthirsty and wanton massacre."

It should be noted that General Miles was not among those who pushed the propaganda. As the US awarded some of the perpetrators of the massacre with Medals of Honor and erected a monument to the cavalry members who died there, Miles pushed for an inquiry. Knowing that there were women and children involved, he was not willing to simply sweep events under the rug. Following the events of Wounded Knee and his role in setting those events in motion, General Miles emerged as a leading champion in the search for justice for the Lakota. He believed that the cavalry had committed unspeakable wrongs against an innocent people.

Given the brutal treatment used by the US government for minor and imaginary infractions by the native peoples, there are some who believe that the troops were sent out specifically to commit genocide. The US had already proved they were not above committing genocide when it came to subduing the native peoples and stealing anything of value that they had. However, the problem with calling it a genocide is that the troops did stop shooting. Some Lakota were left alive.

The fault for the events certainly belongs with the tyrannical relationship, based on misperceptions, that the US had with the native peoples. This sense permeated the ranks of the US military, but there were few solid policies. The president at the time, Ulysses

S. Grant, failed to define the relationship and treatment of the native people. What little guidance was provided followed the well-established repressive and cruel treatment that Europeans had established nearly as soon as they arrived.

However, the tragic events at Wounded Knee have finally come to be known in the US as what it has been called by native people and Europeans for more than 100 years: it was a massacre.

Chapter 17 – Geronimo

One of the most legendary Native Americans is known simply by a single name: Geronimo. The name is associated with doing something courageous, typically jumping off of a cliff or other surface. This is comparable to nursery rhymes because it takes something historical and tragic and dismissively turns it into a cliché. This certainly was not the original intent though.

The man himself is largely a mystery to many people. Apart from recognizing his name, the fact that he was a Native American, and that it is something they scream when jumping, most people could not tell you much about the man himself. Like many native people, his history was tragic, and he became a symbol of the strength and courage of a people up against impossible odds.

A Peaceful Start Changes into a Nightmare

The Apache were a notable nomadic tribe that lived in the Southwestern region, but by the time Geronimo was born, they had become more peaceful than their ancestors had been. This could have been because of the Spanish and those of Spanish descent who had killed so many of the natives.

In June of 1829, a baby boy was born in what is now No-doyohn Canyon, Arizona. At the time, this was still part of the Mexican territory. The fourth child born to his parents, there would be four more children born after him, totaling eight children (four boys and four girls). The new baby was named Goyathlay, or "One Who

Yawns." The first 17 years of his life were largely uneventful. After his 17th birthday, he joined the Council of the Warriors, which gave him the right to finally marry. He soon wed an Apache woman by the name of Alope. By the 1850s they had had three children.

Up to this point in Geronimo's life, the Apache had lived in relative peace with few problems from the Mexicans who lived near them. The tribe was moving along during the summer of 1858. Traveling first from Sonora to Casa Grande, they made a few stops. One was in a town commonly called Kas-ki-yeh by the natives. As it was a Mexican town, they camped outside of it, remaining several days as they traded with the citizens of the town and rested. Some of the Apache warriors would remain behind to protect the camp while others went into the town to trade and get more goods. The men who stayed behind were armed and protected the women and children in the camp.

After a few largely uneventful days, the men were returning from Kas-ki-yeh when they encountered a few women and children fleeing the camp. They soon learned that Mexican troops from a different town had attacked the camp, killing all of the guards and some women and children, including Geronimo's wife, three children, and mother. The Mexican soldiers stole their horses and goods, destroying whatever they did not want or could not take with them.

The warrior council that he had joined at the age of 17 had not convened for anything serious since he had become a member, but now they had a reason to meet and reach a course of action in retaliation for what had happened. With only eight warriors left, Geronimo did not give his voice either for or against any particular action. They had no supplies, no weapons, and still a few women and children who required protection in what was now clearly enemy territory. The Apache chief decided that the best course of action was to leave the camp as the soldiers had left it, including the bodies of the dead where they lay, and to return to their home as quickly and silently as they could.

While many members of his tribe had lost relatives, he was the only one to have lost his entire family when the Mexicans massacred the peaceful tribe. For several days Geronimo did not react. He did not hunt or eat as he was nearly paralyzed with grief. It took several days of forced marches before they reached home, by which time he had started to eat and talk with others about what had happened. Upon reaching his home, Geronimo was met with the decorations his wife had left and the toys of his children. His father had already died, so he visited the grave, the only family grave he could visit, after burning both his home and that of his mother. All of his past was destroyed as he came to terms with the fact that the life he had known was over. He could not give his wife, mother, or children a proper burial, and his peaceful life turned into a strong desire to get revenge on those who had destroyed everything he had known.

From the day that he first began grieving, Geronimo hated all Mexicans. It would be the Mexicans who gave him the name Geronimo, which was the Spanish version of Jerome.

Rise of a Formidable Opponent

Like a phoenix, the Geronimo who existed after the fires of his home and his mother's home was a completely new person. As the council met, they took stock of their weapons and began to plan war with Mexico. Geronimo's first role was to gain assistance from their Apache neighbors. He recorded his recollection of his appeal for aid:

> Kinsman, you have heard what the Mexicans have recently done without cause…we can do to them what they have done to us. Let us go forward and trail them—I will lead you to their city—we will attack them in their homes. I will fight in the front of the battle—I only ask you to follow me to avenge this wrong done by these Mexicans…If I am killed no one need mourn for me. My people have all been killed in that country, and I, too, will die if need be.

The appeal won over the warriors of the first tribe and then the second.

Roughly a year passed as they planned and prepared. During the summer of 1859, the Apache tribes were on the warpath. Starting at the Mexican border, they looked formidable with their faces painted and their weapons ready. The Apaches who were not part of the fight were hidden in the mountains to protect them from retaliation.

When they reached their destination, the town sent out a small group of eight men to parley with the Apache. All eight were killed and scalped. The Mexican troops came out in response, and there were minor skirmishes that lasted for the day. The Apaches were successful in taking over a supply train, giving them more weapons and provisions. The next morning, the Mexican town sent their own force: two units of cavalry and two infantry units. Geronimo recognized the people from the town who had killed his family in one of the cavalry units. Requesting permission to lead the Apache against the cavalry, the chieftains granted the request, despite the fact that Geronimo had no battle experience.

He sent those under his lead to create a hollow circle around the advancing cavalry. As the cavalry attacked Geronimo and his men in the front, other Apache warriors closed in from behind. The battle lasted two hours, and only four Apaches remained when it ended; none of the cavalry survived. Soldiers from another fight soon attacked them, killing two of the remaining Apache warriors. Geronimo and the other survivor attempted to flee, but his companion was cut down. Geronimo turned and killed the first attacker with a spear. The second he killed with a knife, despite the man having a saber. As other Apaches saw the single survivor taking down not only the cavalry soldiers but also striking down soldiers from another division, they began to shout the Apache war-whoop. After his fierce actions, Geronimo became the war chief of his tribe. One of his first orders was to scalp all of the slain Mexicans.

They then continued to raid and attack Mexican settlements along the northern border of Mexico.

A New Enemy

The Mexican troops were no match for the fierce warrior they had created. Geronimo found numerous successes as he led his people against settlements on the border, but a new enemy was encroaching on their ancestral lands—the Americans.

During the 1870s, the US government was actually able to strike a peaceful balance with the Apache. Lieutenant Colonel George F. Crook was able to maintain the peace for as long as it was his responsibility. Unfortunately, his successors were not nearly so adept or competent. In 1876, the US government decided that they preferred to move the Apache fighters, called Chiricahua, to a reservation that was in a completely barren wasteland that the US knew it would not want to occupy. When the Apache found that the lands were not only impossible for living in their traditional ways but also that the US government also failed to make good on the required rations that would allow the Apache to survive, the Apache revolted.

Fleeing the reservation, Geronimo led hundreds of his people into Mexico. Instead of raiding Mexican towns, they turned their attention to the American settlers who were stealing their ancestral lands. The raids lasted for 10 years.

General Crook was sent back to deal with the Apache, this time to force them back to the reservation. This started a pattern for the Apache of escaping the poor conditions of the reservation and surrendering to the military and being taken back to the reservation. Never trusting any of the agreements of the US government that had repeatedly proven that it was untrustworthy, Geronimo led his people away when things were too difficult for them to remain where they were.

In 1886, General Miles was in charge of the American soldiers in the area. When he met Geronimo, he promised the distinguished chief that he and his Apache brethren would be sent to Florida for an indefinite exile, but would then be returned to Arizona. As could be expected, this was a lie, and the men were forced to do hard labor instead of imprisonment. When he was released, Geronimo was sent to Oklahoma instead of Arizona. The pattern of escape and surrender continued, partly because Geronimo could not assimilate into the artificial life that the American government tried to force on him.

A Legend and a Curiosity

By the 1880s and 90s, Geronimo was one of the most famous Native Americans in the US and Mexico. He had become an interesting celebrity, and his ferocity was largely exaggerated with many people claiming he was bulletproof (considering how many raids and battles he had survived, it was an understandable mistake). He joined other Native Americans who were in Wild West Shows. Other native peoples who had been in the show included Chief Joseph, Sitting Bull, and Rains in the Face. These men used the shows as a way of traveling the lands that belonged to their peoples and other natives all across the US. They were also taken to Europe to tour, which proved to be an interesting and eye-opening experience for the native peoples.

For President Theodore Roosevelt's 1905 inaugural parade, Geronimo was invited to attend and joined the president. This led to further interest and curiosity in the legendary Apache warrior who had survived so much. Geronimo was easily one of the most popular figures because of his legendary reputation. Long before cell phones made selfies popular, people clamored to get their pictures taken with the legendary Apache warrior. In 1906 his memoirs were published: *Geronimo's Story of His Life*. Despite having traveled all over the world, he did not get to return to his ancestral land. He succumbed to pneumonia just after Valentine's Day in 1909. He was buried in Fort Sill, Oklahoma, along with the other Apaches who died so far from their homes.

Chapter 18 – The Famous Will Rogers

It is incredibly easy to look at the way Native Americans were treated and to feel that the situation is depressing and hopeless. However, there are plenty of examples of descendants turning the tragic histories into stories of triumph. One of the most interesting examples of this is the famous humorist, performer, and journalist, Will Rogers. He is an example of just how much descendants can do to help open the eyes of others to the plight of the Native Americans and to remind everyone that a person is a person, regardless of their origins.

It is fascinating how many people have heard of Will Rogers, and the name conjures up smiles because he was both funny and poignant. A well-respected actor, he was born at a time that was among the darkest in US history. He proved that despite everything, there was always a way to find success.

Born in Privilege in Native American Territory

Will Rogers was not born into the poverty and hardships that are usually associated with Native Americans. On November 4, 1879, William Penn Adair Rogers was welcomed into the home of Clement and Mary Rogers. As the baby of the family (the eighth child), he had a slightly easier life than his older siblings. His parents were also wealthy for the time, even though they lived near Claremore, Oklahoma, territory that still belonged to the Native

Americans. While his father had been an extremely successful farmer and rancher, leading to success as a businessman and politician, Will Rogers himself was a quarter Cherokee (one of his grandparents had been full-blooded Cherokee). He grew up comfortably talking to both Americans and the Native Americans who lived near him.

He was an incredibly affable young man who was very close with his mother. Given that both Will and his father had very strong personalities, they had a more contentious relationship. The family suffered a tragic loss when Will was just 10 years old and his mother died. This was an event that shaped his life and his future.

Finding Purpose Well Outside the Norm

Will was not ignorant of the wrongs done to the native peoples, and he felt that his unique blend of Caucasian and Native American blood, coupled with his early life in the west made, him an ideal American citizen. He spent some years working on the ranch, but left for South Africa when he was still a teenager. Having gone nearly half-way around the world, Rogers soon found that he was very adept at performing.in Wild West shows. Because he had grown up on a ranch and had a southern drawl, he was easily able to act like a cowboy.

He returned to the US and traveled with the circus and other Wild West shows. Finally, he landed in one of the roles for which he is best known, a vaudeville actor. This was an incredibly natural progression, and in 1905 he proved to be hugely popular as he executed incredibly difficult tricks with a lasso while making humorous quips.

From vaudeville, he easily transitioned to Broadway where his humor and take on life were wildly popular. Rogers had an innate charisma that was often found among Cherokee leaders, as well as an intellect and understanding of how people worked. He used his abilities to entertain and presented his philosophies in a way that charmed and intrigued audiences. His shows often included humor, for which he would become famous, and his personal take on the latest news.

A Failed Promise and a Better Calling

Although Rogers had never really wanted for anything because of his family's wealth, he had lived in harsher conditions by choice. What he earned was based solely on his own abilities and affability. The outstanding and humorous shows on Broadway opened doors for him into the new world of film. Rogers soon moved his wife and children to California where he became a leading man in silent films. His first role was in *Laughing Bill Hyde* which was released in 1918. Ironically, the quips and humor for which he had been known so clearly could not be translated to silent film. However, he had also spent a lot of time performing intricate tricks in the Wild West shows, which easily translated into amazing performances on the screen.

Rogers had originally been signed to a contract for two years, but when the studio management changed, his contract was terminated. He attempted to start his own production company, but it was unsuccessful. After such a promising future was cut short, he returned with his family to New York City where he rejoined the Ziegfeld Follies.

Perhaps unsatisfied with a life he had already tried, Rogers published collections called *The Cowboy Philosopher on the Peace Conference* and *The Cowboy Philosopher on Prohibition*. The books were published in 1919 and gave him a way to move into a different field. Rogers had found a niche that reached the common people as prohibition led to things like the rise of organized crime and speakeasies. He was an incredibly popular figure during the Roaring 20s, as he poked fun at everyone. No politician or person of note was spared from his quips.

Outside of his publications and public persona, he was actually on incredibly good terms with the very people that he made fun of in his shows. Rogers was on equally good terms with the politicians who drew his unique sense of humor. At one point, he wanted the following words inscribed on his tombstone: "I joked about every prominent man of my time, but I have never met a man I didn't like."

There were some extreme downsides to his incredibly gregarious and affable nature. And like his ancestors, he wasn't always a good judge of character as he at one point publicly supported the brutal dictator Benito Mussolini. It is possible that he did not know exactly how Mussolini controlled his country as the US at the time tended to avoid paying attention to events occurring outside of the US in their quest for isolation.

He used his humor and charm to become a journalist with a syndicated column. This was an obvious natural progression from his publications but a significant distance from where he started as a small player in Wild West shows in South Africa. Rogers started his column in 1922, published in *The Illiterate Digest*. The humor that he displayed early on to criticize the US government soon grew into commentary on the world stage. Following the end of World War I, he openly pushed for world disarmament. This helped to push him onto the international stage, and he was sent to Europe by the *Saturday Evening Post*. His writings from this period were compiled into a collection called *Letters of a Self-Made Diplomat to His President*, who at the time was Calvin Coolidge. His time in Europe ended in a visit to Russia, which resulted in his collection called *There's Not a Bathing Suit in Russia*. The country had claimed to be a Communist country but was actually under the control of the ruthless dictator Stalin. His 1927 publication discussed what life was like when the government controlled everything and rationed it to the people.

Having found little success in films, Rogers still understood the value of a more widespread medium—and at that time, radio was in the early stages. Rogers's first radio broadcast occurred in 1926, and he proved to be just as much of a draw as he had been on Broadway and the Wild West shows before that. By 1930, he had his own weekly show. Given his roots, Rogers chose to use his large platform to draw attention to humanitarian issues; he had seen many instances both inside the US and around the world that concerned him. For example, in 1927, the Mississippi River overran its banks in many places, causing devastating floods. He went to these regions himself to see what he could do and then went to testify before Congress about how horrible the disaster was. He wanted Congress to provide more aid to the region to help with recovery efforts.

Following Black Monday and the start of the Great Depression in 1929, Rogers soon backed the ideas of President Franklin D. Roosevelt. When the New Deal was enacted in 1933, he fully supported it. He also held benefits and personally acted to try to help those devastated during the Great Depression. In 1935, he was traveling to the USSR with a friend, the pilot of the small plane taking them there. It crashed in Alaska, killing both of the men.

A Lasting Legacy

Will Rogers was an incredibly unique individual. His entire life was spent balancing between two completely different worlds, yet it was a balancing act that he was solely able to maintain. While poking fun at those in power, he also befriended them. He was a man of the people, but larger than life. His sense of humor was biting, but helped call attention to things that could be improved. Though Rogers was critical, he also offered solutions. He lived through some of the worst chapters in American history, and saw some of the worst of humanity, yet he chose to remain optimistic and pressed for positive change. Today his words are still published and readily available (even on Kindle), and they are still as poignant, biting, applicable, and stubbornly optimistic as they were when he first wrote them.

Chapter 19 – The Unbreakable Code of the Code Talkers

Stories about World War II show that it was a very perilous time, one that threatened to tear the world apart as the two "civilized" continents of Europe and Asia tried to conquer the whole world. People from all around the world were drawn into the conflict to deny the thirst for power by the Axis Powers. The main aggressors—Germany, Japan, and Italy—had managed to take control of disproportionately large areas compared to their own geographically-small countries. They seemed to be better organized, more knowledgeable about their enemies' movements, and had superior arms. Country after country fell to their attacks, making them seem impossible to defeat.

Ultimately, it was some Native Americans who helped turn the tide in a war that should have had nothing to do with them. The destruction of Europe and Asia should have been unimportant; this was not their fight. However, they proved once again that Native Americans were much more than the peoples that the US had portrayed them as being for centuries.

Joining the War

Canada joined World War II as Adolf Hitler became an obvious threat to more than just a few countries on the European continent. Although they were their own country, Canada still had strong ties with England. The US, however, wanted to avoid being drawn into another war after all of their losses during World War I. The Second World War had been raging since the end of the 1930s, but the US only joined after the bombing of Pearl Harbor by Japan in December of 1941.

Just as they had in World War I, Native Americans began to sign up to join the ranks of the US military to help protect their people. What has long been misunderstood about the native peoples is that the word "warriors" was never really an accurate term to describe the people who went to war. It is an English word that settlers applied to the people they fought against because the settlers failed to understand the significance of the role that the native men assumed when they joined the battle; they were protectors first and foremost. Their goal was always to ensure that their people survived through whatever means necessary, including a warrior's death during battle. However, the term warrior implies that they were basically a type of soldier. In truth, the native warriors were negotiators, farmers, and whatever else was needed to help the people. They were well respected not just because of their bravery, but also for their strength, courage, and intellect. This was the mindset of the Native Americans who joined the US military during both World War I and World War II. These wars were an apparent threat to their people and they responded. Roughly a quarter of the Native American population volunteered in World War I. Of the estimated 350,000 natives remaining at the time the US joined World War II, about 44,000 served in the military. Although the Native Americans should have been immune to the draft since the US government had made it clear for more than 100 years that the natives weren't American, some were still forced into service through the draft. However, many volunteered. Expecting to be put on the front lines to fight, they soon found that their ability to speak their people's language meant that some of them would have a completely different role in the war.

The Hunt for an Unbreakable Code

One of the biggest problems for both sides was the theft of military instructions. Given the scale of the war, coordinating military action was incredibly difficult, and the two sides were constantly spying on each other to get the information they needed to know about what the other side was planning and have time to counter it.

The Germans developed the Enigma Code, which was called unbreakable. This actually appeared to be true for most of the war because the messages that they transmitted were unintelligible without the use of an Enigma Machine. The first machine was created in the early 1900s and was patented in 1919. Over the years it was integrated into the German military, and they continued to make changes and tweaks to it to hide their classified information from the other side during transmissions. Following the invasion of Poland, the British gained some intelligence on the code that the Germans had been using for more than a decade. Still, the Germans were constantly changing the code, and the only way to know what was being said was by having an actual machine. The British finally got their hands on two of the machines in 1941 when they captured a German trawler. From those machines, they were able to postulate where the main sources of the code originated so that they could follow the messages. The Germans realized that they had been compromised by the end of the year and added updates to their machines to include another layer of code. The problem was that the codes could be deciphered with the right level of effort and some luck to capture the right vehicles carrying the machines.

The US saw how much time and effort the British had been putting into deciphering the Enigma Code and realized they needed something much more secure to protect their military communications. Some Japanese spies in the US were taking information and passing it to the Japanese government, which had resulted in heavy casualties for the Americans sent to fight on the other side of the world. During World War I, some Native Americans were assigned the task of transmitting messages in their native tongues. Philip Johnston remembered how the Choctaw he had worked with had successfully relayed plans during that war. Despite being Caucasian, Johnston had been raised on the Navajo reservation, and it was his suggestion to use the Navajo to communicate in their native tongue to counter the Japanese spies. Following an impressive demonstration by the Navajo, the Marines recruited 29 members of the tribe. Their main goal was to use their native tongue to develop a code that would be impossible to translate without knowing the Navajo language. Two weeks later, the code was ready. From this, a Code Talkers school was created to train more people, since by then the war spanned the entire globe and 29 people would not be enough. Some of the Code Talkers were drafted (they were part Caucasian), others volunteered, and a number of them lied about their age, with the youngest being only 15 years old when he volunteered. A total of 16 Native American tribes joined the coding effort.

Different Levels of Coding

Not only did the military and the Code Talkers develop a code based on the many different Native American languages, they used different levels based on the importance of a message. For minor transmissions, the native people simply relayed a message in their native tongue, knowing that there was no way for the Axis Powers to interpret even the encoded messages.

The training for the coded portions of the transmissions was staggeringly easy for the Native Americans as well. Some of the Caucasian Code Talkers were in awe of how quickly the native people could learn and accurately execute their knowledge. The code was based on the Navajo language since they were the ones who came up with the code. However, they used something that all Native Americans were familiar with as the basis for the code— North American animals. They assigned animals to each of the

English letters for the code. After this, they needed to come up with ways of communicating military and technical ideas that were not part of their native tongue, such as airplane and tank. For this part, Native Americans relied on their own languages to come up with the codes, which meant that the code based on Navajo would not be easily translated by Comanche Code Talkers since they would translate the English they were given into their native tongues as part of the code. While there are similarities between Comanche and Navajo, they are not the same language, just as Spanish is not the same as Portuguese, Italian, or French. If you had a native Spanish speaker and a native French speaker to translate the same English text into their native tongues, they would not be able to decode each other's messages unless they knew the other language as well.

There were Code Talkers stationed at command centers but that also meant that there had to be some Code Talkers on the battlefield. They were in constant peril like all of the other soldiers, yet like their forefathers, they proved that they were able to keep a level head and complete their missions while the world was exploding (sometimes literally) around them. The Code Talkers were given the message they needed to relay in English. They would turn around and mentally translate the entire thing either into their native tongue or into the code. The speed at which they could do this was mesmerizing, but as one Native American reminded the soldier who asked about it, many of the Native American languages were not written languages. All of their histories had been passed down through oral traditions for millennia: "we listen, we hear, we learn to remember everything. It's part of our training," said Carl Gorman of the US Marine Corps, Navajo Code Talkers. Applying that deep understanding of language to transmitting code was little different than speaking was for most Americans.

The Code Talkers were sent to different regions based on their language. The Hopi and Navajo were sent to the Pacific where their code baffled the Japanese. The Comanches primarily countered the Enigma Code of the Germans with their superior unbreakable code.

The Meskwakis were assigned to fight in the regions of Northern Africa where Germany and Italy had a tentative foothold. The remaining Code Talkers were assigned more specific duties as there were fewer of them and the US tried to use the valuable resource with caution. Code Talkers were present for many of the major turning points of the war. One Comanche Code Talker, Charles Chibitty, spoke of his experience: "Utah Beach in Normandy was something else. Everybody asked me if I would go through it again, and I said, no, but I could train the younger ones how we used our language and let them go ahead and do it because it was hell." Some became prisoners of war, and they suffered alongside the other Americans and prisoners in foreign lands. Many of them recount how they kept faith and prayed to get through the ordeal, just as the other soldiers prayed to their gods.

Ultimately, the work of the Code Talkers saved thousands of allied lives. Their ability to quickly translate English into their tongue and code, then quickly decipher it under some of the most horrific situations, was awe-inspiring and not something that any of the enemies could have anticipated. Even if the Axis Powers had anticipated it, they did not have the means to translate it. The US was the only place where these native peoples resided, and their numbers were incredibly small.

The Navajo made their own dictionary of the code that they developed, and it was kept secret by the US military until 1968. The dictionary is now available for viewing and shows just how inventive and clever the Code Talkers were in a war that was far from their homes. If anyone had a reason to avoid the war, it was the Native Americans. Their ancestors were so far removed from Asia that it was only a legend about how they reached their home, and any possible roots to Europe were just as ancient. For them, their home was the place where their ancestors had lived for thousands of years. Yet, they still went into the uncertainty of a war that was not theirs to fight.

Conclusion

Tens of thousands of years before Europeans began to stumble upon the continents of North and South America, the indigenous peoples had developed many rich and complex cultures based on the areas where they resided. The people of South and Central America tended toward more structured social hierarchies. The indigenous people of North American tended to stay close to nature and many remained more mobile, chasing after the big game of their respective lands. There were also many peoples who had established themselves in areas that were rich in natural resources, particularly along both of the coasts. North America has one of the most diverse range of climates on the planet, and the people reflected just how much humanity had to adapt to survive in the different terrains. To the north were freezing lands that were harsh, and the people were hardy and adaptable. Along the coasts, the lands had all of the necessary resources for easy survival. As a result, the people had developed a more lavish lifestyle and more structured societies. The chiefs also had a much larger population to manage as they created nations and confederations. The areas between the Appalachian and Cascade Mountain Ranges included deserts, plains, a large plateau, and salt lakes. As a result, the people in these regions had adjusted to survive under some very unique circumstances.

Although there were many languages, primary language families were making it possible for natives to communicate in much the same way as those in Europe did near the borders of the adjoining countries. Written language, though, was uncommon on much of the

North American continent, which means millennia of history and heritage were not recorded.

With the arrival of the Europeans, everything changed. The histories and heritages of the people have largely been lost or overwritten from the perspective of the settlers and their descendants. Having to look at the rich and complex peoples through such a narrow lens would be like trying to define the history of Europe by an invading and conquering people from a completely different continent. The descendants of the native peoples have maintained their own perspective, but they have been the victims of US policy of removal and genocide, their cultures have been ignored, and the propaganda largely broadcast by the invaders.

The role that the Canadian government played against the native peoples in the northern regions has also been largely ignored. There were Native Americans who attempted to flee to Canada (some successfully) from the US because their policies were far less cruel than the policies of the US. Had the US failed to win the War for Independence, you can look to Canada to see how the natives would have been treated under the crown. They were clearly against genocide, looking down on both the Spanish and the Americans for the way they treated the native peoples. Great Britain and Canada's approach was more of a "civilized" displacement, forcing people off of their native lands, constantly pushing them into smaller and smaller pockets of land. Today the natives in Canada are impoverished and still find it difficult to assimilate despite racism being more tempered but still very much present. As it was far less populous than the lands to the south in the US, there were also far fewer people to displace. Although the indigenous people were certainly treated better (an unbelievably low bar to set as it is being compared to genocide), the natives were expected to give up their way of life. It should be noted that Canada has actually done more to acknowledge the native peoples and their contributions, and they do attempt to live together, but the racism and bias against the native peoples has proven to be a large stumbling block for a nation renowned for being friendly.

Perhaps the largest problem is the refusal of both the US and Canada to acknowledge the horrors that they committed against the native peoples. Often the excuse of "that was a long time ago" is put forward, but that is clearly not true. The recent events at places like Standing Rock (where a Native American protest occurred against the Dakota Access Pipeline) prove that neither country is willing to change their policies that have been around for centuries; they will not do the right thing for the native peoples if it means the difference in making a profit. The people involved in the protests at Standing Rock are the people of Sitting Bull, Crazy Horse, and many other notable Sioux people. Living on the reservations promised them by the US government, they are again having their resources put at risk by a pipeline that will provide little for anyone outside of a few of the wealthy. Nor is it only a problem with the US government; the XL pipeline is part of a project by a Canadian company. Originally, the course of the pipeline would have taken it past a region that was populated by white people. As a result, the Canadian company changed the path to put the native peoples at risk in the event that there is a problem with the pipeline. This blatant disregard for the peoples that both countries have wronged shows that their continued refusal to acknowledge the wrongs of the past means they will continue to perpetrate wrongs against Native Americans. Just as there were many Americans and Canadians against the wrongs committed by their governments, the protests have seen an influx of Caucasians willing to finally stand with the Native Americans to try to force the governments to do the right thing. This effort fails to acknowledge the much wider wrongs, but it is a start that if moved forward could finally see the changes needed to stop the barbaric treatment against the indigenous peoples.

Despite all of the horrors and suffering, Native Americans have proven to be incredibly adaptable and optimistic. They have aided the US and Canada during times when they could easily have refused to help. Without the involvement of the Navajo to communicate military plans, it is highly unlikely that the US would have seen the kinds of success they experienced during World War II prior to the use of nuclear weapons. Descendants of the native peoples, such as Will Rogers, have shown that they are able to turn their skills and intellect to better use. If the US and Canadian governments were to actually begin to atone for the wrongs committed since the first settlers arrived, it would help prevent such horrors in the future.

Bibliography

10 Facts About the Bold, Brave Life of Sacagawea: Ryleigh Nucilli, 2018, Ranker, **ranker.com**

A History of Western Eating Utensils, From the Scandalous Fork to the Incredible Spork: Lisa Bramen, July 31, 2009, Smithsonian.com

Aboriginal History in Canada: Indigenous and Northern Affairs Canada, 2018, Government of Canada, **www.aadnc-aandc.gc.ca/**

An Introduction to North America's Native People: 2015, **native-langauges.org**

Arctic Indians: Linda Alchen, January 16, 2018, **infolinks.com**

Bering Strait Myth: John Teohawks, Native Circle

Biographies of Plains Indians – Crazy Horse – 1842-1877: American Indian Relief Council, 2018, **nativepartnership.org**

Biographies of Plains Indians – Sitting Bull – 1831 -1890: American Indian Relief Council, 2018, **nativepartnership.org**

Blackhawk Museum - Sitting Bull: Blackhawk Museum, 2018, **blackhawkmuseum.org**

Breaking Germany's Enigma Code: Andrew Lycett, February 17, 2011, BBC History, **bbc.co.uk**

California Cultures: Native Americans: University of California, 2005, **calisphere.org**

California Native Americans: Linda Alchen, January 1, 2018, Siteseen Limited

California Slaughter: The State-Sanctioned Genocide of Native Americans: Alexander Nazaryn, August 17, 2016, News Week LLC, **newsweek.com**

Canada's First Peoples: Goldi Productions, 2007, **firstpeopleofcanada.com**

Culture Areas, Tribes: American Indians' Cultural Network, 2000, **american-indians.net**

First Humans Entered the Americas along the Coast, Not through the Ice: Jason Daley, August 11, 2016, **Smithsonian.com**

Geronimo – Goyathlay ("one who yawns"): 2015, **indians.org**

Geronimo – The Last Apache Holdout: 2018, **legendsofamerica.com**

Geronimo His Own Story: George M. Welling, 2012, **let.rug.nl**

Great Basin Indians: Linda Alchen, January 1, 2018, Siteseen Limited

Great Plains Indians: American Indians' Cultural Network, 2000, **american-indians.net**

Hiawatha: Facts, information and articles about Hiawatha, a Native American Indian Chief from Wild West: 2018, **historynet.com**

Hiawatha: Linda Alchen, January 1, 2018, Siteseen Limited

History of the Bering Land Bridge Theory: National Park Service, March 16, 2018

Indian Resistance and Removal: Seminole Tribe of Florida, 2018, **semtribe.com**

Indians and the American Revolution: Wilcomb E. Washburn, 2014-2017, The JDN Group, LLC

Infinity of Nations – Arctic / Subarctic: National Museum of the American Indian, **nmai.si.edu**

Leif Eriksson: History Channel, 2018, A&E Television Networks

Native American Cultures: History Channel, 2018, A&E Television Networks

Native American Faces: Sacagawea: 2018, **thewildwest.org**

Native American Indian Facts – Great Plains American Indian Facts: **native-american-indian-facts.com**

Native American Indian Facts – Plateau American Indian Facts: **native-american-indian-facts.com**

Native Americans of the Northeast Woodlands: The-Crankshaft Publishing, **what-when-how.com/**

Native Americans Tribes and Regions: Ducksters, June 13, 2018, Technological Solutions, Inc

Native Americans: Native Americans: Indian Tribes of North America, Gaston County Public Library, August 13, 2016

Native Heritage Project: March 9, 2012, **nativeheritageproject.com**

Native Tribes and Languages of the Arctic: 2015, **native-langauges.org**

Native Words Native Warriors: Edwin Schupman, 2018, National Museum of the American Indian, **nmai.si.edu**

Northwest Coast Indians: 2018, **indians.org**

Northwest Coast Native Americans: Linda Alchen, January 1, 2018, Siteseen Limited

Other Migration Theories – Bering Land Bridge National Preserve: National Park Service

Plateau Indians: Linda Alchen, January 1, 2018, Siteseen Limited

Pocahontas Revealed: WGBH Educational Foundation, 2007, **pbs.org**

Roanoke Colony Deserted: History Channel, 2018, A&E Television Networks

Roanoke Island: North Carolina History Projects, 2018, **carolinahistory.web.unc.edu/**

Southeast Native Americans: Siteseen Limited, January 1, 2018, **www.warpaths2peacepipes.com**

Southwest Indians: 2018, **indians.org**

Southwest Native American: Linda Alchen, January 1, 2018, Siteseen Limited

Standing Rock Sioux Tribe: Standing Rock Sioux Tribe, 2018, **standingrock.org**

Subarctic People: Goldi Productions, 2007, **firstpeopleofcanada.com**

Tatanka-Iyotanka (aka Sitting Bull): Omeka, 2018, **lib.umich.edu**

The Death of the Bering Strait Theory: Alexander Ewen, August 12, 2016, Indian Country Today

The Great Basin Tribes: Objwa, March 17, 2012, **nativeamericannetroots.net**

The Interpreter's Wife: Gary E. Moulton, 2018, **lewis-clark.org**

The Lost Colony A Local Legacy: America Story, The Library of Congress, **americaslibrary.gov**

The Seminole Wars: Seminole Nation Museum, 2012, **seminolenationmuseum.org**

The True Story of Pocahontas: Jackie Mansky, March 23, 2017, Smithsonian.com

The True Story of Thanksgiving: Patrick J. Kiger, 2018, National Geographic, **nationalgeographic.com**

The True Story of the First Thanksgiving: Scott Craven, November 21, 2017, **azcentral.com**

The Truth about the Wounded Knee Massacre: Patti Jo King, December 30, 2016, Indian Country Today

We Are the Land: Native American Views of Nature: Booth A.L., 2003, Springer International Publishing AG

We Finally Have Clues to How the Lost Roanoke Colony Vanished: History Channel, 2018, A&E Television Networks

What happened to the "Lost Colony" of Roanoke?: History Channel, OCTOBER 02, 2012, A&E Television Networks

What Native American Language Diversity Tells Us, Highpine, Gayle, April, 24, 2016.

Who Were the First Americans?: National Geographic, September 3, 2003

Will Rogers Biography - Film Actor, Actor (1879-1935): Biography, April 27, 2017, A&E Television Networks, **biography.com**

Will Rogers Biography: Encyclopedia of World Biography, 2018, Advameg Inc., **notablebiographies.com**

Wind Talkers: Navajo Code Talkers in WWII: Bos Carole, November 9, 2018, **awesomestories.com**

Free Bonus from Captivating History (Available for a Limited time)

Hi History Lovers!

Now you have a chance to join our exclusive history list so you can get your first history ebook for free as well as discounts and a potential to get more history books for free! Simply visit the link below to join.

Captivatinghistory.com/ebook

Also, make sure to follow us on:

Twitter: @Captivhistory

Facebook: Captivating History:@captivatinghistory